ARCHITECTURAL MODELS
CONSTRUCTION TECHNIQUES

WOLFGANG KNOLL AND MARTIN HECHINGER

WITH 208 PHOTOGRAPHS BY HANS-JOACHIM HEYER

Translated from the German by R.M.E. Diamant

B.T. Batsford Ltd • London

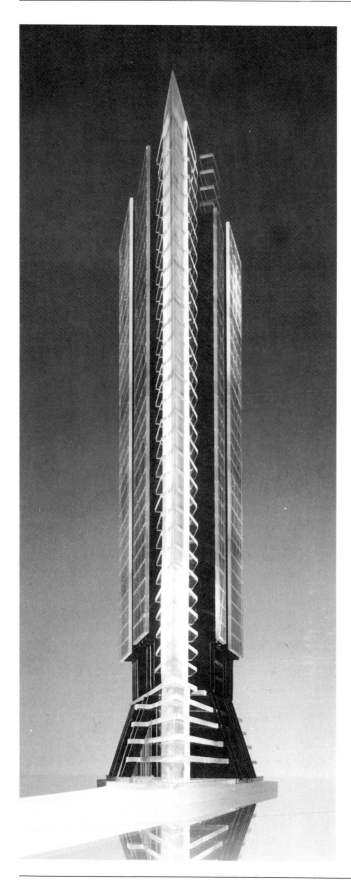

1 Tower office block, Frankfurt, 1:500. Compare fig. 151

First published 1990 by Julius Hoffmann Verlag GmbH, Stuttgart

This edition published 1992

Typeset by Graphicraft Typesetters Ltd, Hong Kong and printed in Great Britain by Butler & Tanner Ltd, Frome, Somerset

Published by
B.T. Batsford Ltd
4 Fitzhardinge Street
London W1H OAH

A CIP catalogue record for this book is available from the British Library

ISBN 0 7134 7102 6

Contents

Preface

Architecture is not only *created* in the form of drawings and models, but it is also largely *presented* to the public in the form of such media. I lecture, supervise experimental work and run seminars in the field of architectural presentation in Department 1: Institute of Architectural Presentation and Design of the University of Stuttgart. This course puts considerable emphasis on the construction of models. Students learn about the techniques and materials to be used, how to transform drawings into models, and how the design may be represented by the model. They learn how to treat the model as a kind of design development in which the building structure can be drafted and examined in sculpture form. They are shown how spatial relationships can be built up and how their varying effects may be controlled. The model complements the drawing and has its own characteristics.

Both the student and the trained architect are able to show the individual style of their work, not only in the form of a drawing, but also in model form.

Following the advice of Kurt Hoffmann, we decided to gather together our work experience and the ample teaching material available, in the form of this book. It was not my intention simply to produce a collection of recipes. The emphasis lies in giving the reader ideas and guidance. Suggestions are also made regarding the way the construction of the model should be viewed as an overall design exercise. This should go well beyond the basic representation of an architectural plan.

We are deeply grateful to Kurt Hoffmann, who gave us advice, helpful criticism and support right from the beginning. Our thanks are also due to Robert Bosch GmbH for supplying us with some model-making machines.

Particularly deserving of my gratitude are my colleagues from Department 1: Hans-Joachim Heyer, Director of the photographic workshop, and Susanne Schmidt, who is the Director of the graphic and reprographic workshop. They provided the excellent photographs of the objects produced, photographic documentation, production of illustrations, and general advice within the fields of their own expertise.

I am delighted that this book is going to be published in the English language and I hope that English-speaking readers will be given both pleasure and useful ideas when they build their models.

Stuttgart, 5 September 1991
Professor Wolfgang Knoll, Dipl. Ing.

1 Introduction

The completion of an architectural design is the fulfilment of a specific task. An architect obviously wants to finish the work with intelligence and imagination. This means that the architect's function is not only to provide rooms for specific usage to allow certain activities to take place, but also to consider the overall spatial quality of his or her creation and the way it fits into its surroundings.

An architectural spatial design utilizes a combination of masses, areas and lines. Expressed in architect's terms, it uses solid shapes, planes and rods. The central theme of an architectural design is the way such units are arranged according to their functions, how they are joined, and how they relate to each other. The design can therefore be considered the satisfactory end of a process in which a solution is provided for a given problem. Professor G. Behnisch said in his address on the occasion of the Hugo Hairing prizegiving ceremony: 'The architectural solution of a given problem is always evident at the end of our work but never at the beginning.' (*Der Architekt*, April 1989) This also underlines one of the pitfalls of the provision of an architectural model. It could give specifications at the start of the design process which are too detailed, and therefore threaten the flexibility of the design at a very early stage.

A specific design process is developed using drawings and models. These are the media by which the process of designing the project can be followed through and brought to a successful conclusion. A drawing, although immediately available and capable of instant modification whenever new ideas come along, deals with the graphic elements of area and line only. It is flat and therefore depicts the actual spatial concept of a building only in an abstract way, making its real nature hard to visualize. A model, in contrast, especially a conceptual or work model, constitutes an immediate transformation of all spatial ideas into a concrete object containing the tectonic elements of body, plane and rod.

Architects think, work and even dream in terms of drawings. The model, particularly a conceptual or provisional model which accompanies a sketch, is necessary to enable others to understand the way an architect works. The first conceptual models also cope with the need to be able to alter and modify details, in the same way as can be done on a drawing. Sketches

2 Conceptual and work models made from corrugated cardboard, 1:200

and conceptual models give an insight into the way an architect studies and analyses shapes and their relationship to one another.

The purpose of this book is to explain all this and to suggest the best way of achieving such aims. Claims have been made in many lectures and publications that the computer is now able to replace drawings and models. It is true that architects cannot do without CAD any more. However, at the beginning of the design stage, or in fact at any time, the computer only has a secondary role. It cannot replace the actual material experience,

the physical shape and the build-up of spatial relationships. Neither the computer nor the sketchpad can replace the function of the conceptual model. Drawing and modelling both constitute a way of working out the shape properties of the design, and building up a three-dimensional repertoire. The basis of the contents of this book, as well as the types of models described, is the development of the tectonic elements of solid bodies, flat surfaces, and rods, and their relationship to each other.

The first stage of making a model is the fabrication of solid shapes, flat sheeting and rod units. These are the basic elements used and they have to be made from different materials and in different sizes. When they are combined, they form the three-dimensional model required. At the same time, every model constitutes an individual entity and has its own artistic criteria, which are often quite different to the drawings, or even the finished buildings. The architectural model represents a stage in the design and is a spatial representation of the architect's imagination. Apart from this, the creation of the model is itself a design project, in which the solid shapes, the sheeting and rods, as well as the topographic base into which they are bedded, are formed and set in relationship to each other. The elements of the model can be described and developed according to different properties, themselves dependent upon the design ideas of the architect. These are: shape, size, direction (position), shading, colour, nature of surface. Depending upon these six variables, it may be possible to insert contrasts, either singly, or one over the other. Such contrasts may involve shape, direction and colour, which can be built into the model. Various problems of an architectural nature can often be solved in this way.

There is, however, a problem which has become apparent from architectural competitions and design exercises: a model has its own characteristic properties, and these may often be unrelated to actual architecture. Just like a drawing, a model is an expression of the thought behind a design. When a building is being completed this tends to drift into the background and may even be overlooked. The difference between a model and the actual building can be confusing even for these with experience. The expert who has to make a reasoned judgment can be misled by the appearance

3   Building model, 1:100. Loadbearing frame made from paper-lined EPS. Façade built from coloured paper, methacrylate sheeting, perforated polystyrene sprayed grey; window frames; railings: soldered wire. The various sections of the façade are glued with double-sided adhesive foil onto the loadbearing frame. Existing structure from polystyrene, sprayed grey.

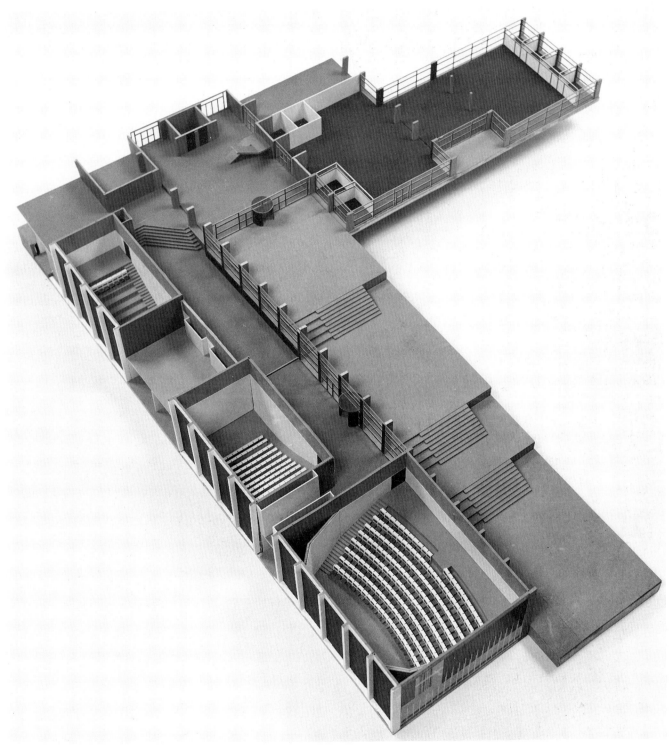

of a model into approving a design which he or she may no longer recognize once the actual building has been completed.

4　Exhibition and work model, 1:50. This model was used to examine different furnishing, colour and material concepts. The base plate consists of 16 mm sandwich timber slab; floors and walls of 5 mm plywood; frame: solid timber; façades: methacrylate sheeting; window frames: methacrylate sheeting and coloured paper.

2 Types of Model

In general, models use solid shapes, flat surfaces and rods as basic elements to represent various items. These are then set up in correlation according to the structure. As an example, the solid basic elements may represent the solid structures in a model of urban construction. On the other hand, the two-dimensional units could constitute the wall or façade surfaces in a sectional model. The rods may represent the supports or frame carriers in a model used for construction purposes. Finally, a combination of all three types of elements is used in a structural or building model. Consequently, it is possible to distinguish between three types of models, depending upon how they are made. There are solid models, models made from plates, and models made by means of rods. There are also numerous transitions between these basic types:

Elements	solids	areas	lines
Tectonic elements	body	plate	rod
Types of models	body-system	plate-system	rod-system
Mutual relationship of elements	body/space body/body body/sheet body/sheet/ rod	plate/space plate/plate plate/rod	rod/space rod/rod body/rod

As can be seen from this table, the initial task of model-making is to fabricate the necessary solid bodies, plates and rods, to shape them, fit them together, and to treat their surfaces. However, it is also possible to use ready-made items by re-interpreting them for inclusion in the model. Alternatively, it is possible to build the entire model using such components as a 'collage'.

If models are to be used for interpretation and analysis, and as a means of developing shapes and their combinations, they may be classified into three groups: topographic models, building models and special models. Topographic models include landscape models, site models and garden models. Building models include town planning models, models of building shells, structural models, internal models and models of build-ing details. Special models can be made of details in design, furnishing and particular objects.

Depending upon the way they are made, models can be classified as body-systems, plate-systems, rod-systems, or the appropriate combination of such systems. In addition, the models may be built for three distinct work stages, with varying needs and different display purposes. For example, as a design aid for students, to give information to a planning committee, for competitive tendering, for an exhibition, or as a show-piece model for the owner of the building.

The models are described in detail as follows:

Topographic models
- Site models (page 12)
- Landscape models (page 13)
- Garden models (page 14)

Models of buildings
- Urban models (page 17)
- Models of actual buildings (page 19)
- Structural models (page 20)
- Internal models (page 21)
- Models of detailed items (page 22)

Special models
- Design models (page 24)
- Furnishing, object models (page 24)

Models are vital at the initial design of the building as they constitute a stage in the drafting process, where modifications or alterations may still be made. The standard building model in its final form only shows this early stage of development. It is only made for presentation purposes to enable the design to be judged. It would be unreasonable to assume that it is in any way identical to the final building. It should therefore be remembered that there is little use for these models at later stages of the planning process. They are seldom employed for operational use or work plans. Detailed models such as, for example, sections of façades or staircases, are useful, as are construction models for the development of alternative jointing methods. Internal room models are used to examine different colour schemes and the visual effect of various materials. Finally, there are viewing models which show historical buildings or stages of construction, as well as models

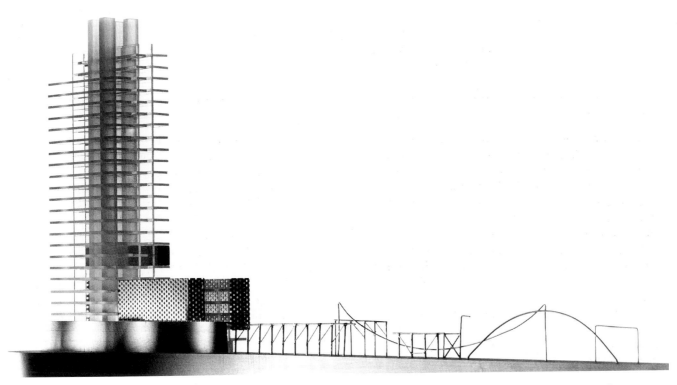

for representation and exhibition purposes.

These models are developed in three stages, relating to the three stages of the design process:

Stage 1: Pre-design   Sketch of ideas
Conceptual model

Stage 2: Design   Design of building
Construction model

Stage 3: Completion   Completion plan
Exhibition model

The requirements of the model differ with every stage of the work. The materials used, the tools employed, and even the place where the work is carried out, may all vary. For example, a model which is used only to represent overall concepts does not require any specialized machinery or workshops. The material to be used must be readily obtainable, easy to shape and to work with. In the case of a construction model, the basic concepts are already fixed. Individual building elements and groups of building elements show distinct characteristics, but they must be readily exchangeable. The purpose of the exhibition model is specific. At this stage the model should be able to interpret the overall design concept. The surfaces and colours used in the model's construction should be fully realistic. The combination of materials and contrasts show up the spatial relationships decided in the overall design clarify them, at times by over-emphasis. Finally, exhibition models have to

5   Building model, 1:500. Transparent methacrylate sheeting level with floors. Core structure from matt ground methacrylate. Façade base: perforated aluminium sheeting, sprayed white. Soldered wire structure. The model shows clearly how solids, areas and rods can be correlated.

include lettering, details of scaling, and orientation (an arrow to indicate the north). It is necessary to plan right from the start how the model should be transported, whether it needs to be taken apart, and how it should be packaged. Depending upon the usage envisaged and materials to be employed, exhibition models may need more sophisticated tools and machines. These, in turn, require improved workshop facilities.

To summarize:

Needs:	Stage of work		
	Conceptual model	Work model	Exhibition model
Material	Easily and quickly obtainable, easily shaped and worked.	Flexible, durable, specialized types often needed.	Durable, stable, light, resistant, capable of being transported.

	Conceptual model	Work model	Exhibition model
Tools	Simple but of good quality. Positioned near drawing board; previous experience not needed.	Ranging from simply to specialized. Practical experience needed. High to very high quality.	Suited to needs of fabrication and type of model. Experience essential. Very high quality.
	All tools should comply with very high safety standards.		
Machines	Rarely or never needed.	Sometimes needed. (Basic equipment); experience necessary.	Specialized machines necessary depending upon type of model; experience essential.
	All machines should comply with very high safety standards.		
Place of work	Drawing table with working surface or work bench next to drawing board.	Work bench with machines connected next to drawing board.	Work bench with machines. Special room desirable.

The following should be easily accessible:

– first aid kit
– safety spectacles
– work benches should have electric power outlets
– workplaces should be well-lit and ventilated.

The following sections describe in greater detail the methods of fabrication, tools and materials needed for topographic models and building structure models.

2.1 Topographic models

The purpose of a topographic model is to represent an existing site plan, to visualize a natural or formalized landscape in a landscape model, or display sections of landscape in a garden model. A model may also represent urban features such as playgrounds, green spaces, parks and cemeteries. Land occupied by squares and roads can be shown both in topographic and building structure models.

Topographic models include the following: planted areas such as trees, groups of trees, woods and bushes; the nature of the terrain, such as rocks, escarpments, undulation, concave and convex sections; traffic areas, green areas and water surfaces; the nature of ground surfaces, such as untreated, asphalted, cobbles, etc.; representation of scale elements, such as urban features, cars and people. Such models are made in scale variations from broad-view to detailed sections, i.e. ranging from about 1:2500 to 1:50.

The site model is generally a strictly-dimensioned representation of the surroundings and the elements mentioned above. It is commonly used as the 'base plate' for the design of buildings. In contrast, landscape and garden models deal with the spatial features of the surroundings. Garden models are usually on a larger scale and show the nature of the plants and structure of the ground. They also indicate the type of ground surface and include features such as the presence of cobbles. Landscape models are always made as modifiable work models, and are themselves a basis for the development of ideas.

2.1.1 Site models

The site model presents a topographic view showing the features of the site and the changes proposed by the new design. It also shows the various built-up areas, traffic areas, green spaces and water surfaces. Trees, groups of trees and escarpments are clearly indicated.

Conceptual model
Conceptual site models with base plate and structure are most unusual. If a site model is made at this stage of the design process it is usually in the form of a work model. The most important requirement is that if the contours of the site are altered the necessary changes on the model can be made without difficulty. With a conceptual model the site may be represented as either a flat or an inclined plane.

Work model
This is a scaled presentation of the shape of the site, indicating the existing paths, as well as specific built-up areas, traffic areas, green spaces and water surfaces. It also shows notable trees and groups of trees. It can be developed further into a exhibition model, but because it is really a work model it must allow for modification to be made.

Exhibition model

This is the final version, showing topography, paths, traffic, green spaces and water areas. Existing and planned trees and groups of trees are included. The quality of fabrication is sufficiently high to satisfy the final use and effect criteria of the model.

2.1.2 Landscape models

This term refers to a representation of the landscape surrounding the site model, using scales of 1:500, 1:1000, 1:2500, and in exceptional cases, 1:5000. In such models, traffic areas, green spaces and water surfaces, as well as all other features, are shown as a simple combination of solid objects. The main purpose of a landscape model is to give an overall impression of the topography of the area. It should indicate specific items such as trees, tree clusters and escarpments, as well as obvious building structures like viewing towers, dams and high-tension masts. Landscape models show housing estates as clusters of solid objects. Such models are needed, for example, for the design of landscape gardens, large parks, garden exhibitions and green areas close to cities.

Conceptual model

As in the case of site models (as work models), landscape models should be developed by simple means. Modifications must be easily accommodated.

Work model

This supplies accurate yet easily modified data of shapes, relationships of space, and sizes. It also gives accurate information on directions and views.

Exhibition model

The task of this model is to give a definitive representation of space and planted areas, and their relationship to existing and planned buildings.

6 Site model as conceptual model. Using bits and pieces such a screws, stones, twigs, machine wire, paper, glue and paper. Gives first impression of the site to enable its shape to be studied. (*top*)

7 Variable subconstruction for site models. Base plate made from roofing timber, covered on both sides with hard fibre sheeting. Drilled in grid modules: 11×11 cm. Rods carrying at their ends 10×10 cm hard fibre plates, fixed by rubber rings high up, are attached to the base plate. The site can be shaped from papier mâché on top of this. (*middle*)

8 Site model made as exhibition model, 1:100. The shape of the site is represented by sloping areas. Terraces are formed by built-up layers; trees from coloured paper, 4 mm plywood, polystyrene, cardboard, wire. (*bottom*)

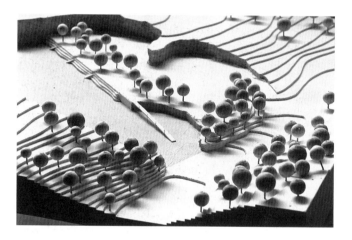

2.1.3 Garden models

This name is given to sections of landscape models, which are larger in scale, namely 1:500, 1:200, 1:100, and exceptionally, 1:50. Such models deal with open areas of smaller housing estates or single buildings, as well as urban internal spaces. The following are indicated: footpaths, study trails, jogging circuits, sports grounds, camping sites, tent sites, facilities for swimming and water sport, allotments, cemeteries, monuments and statues, botanic and zoological gardens, various green spaces, playgrounds, open-air theatres, open-air bathing places, parking areas, historical gardens, terraces and roof gardens, pedestrian precincts, courtyards and squares, viewing towers, ornamental fountains and smaller structures. The main emphasis is, however, given to the modulation of the ground and its physical appearance. This includes types of plants, how squares and paths are formed, fences, walls and gates. Objects which give an impression of the scale used are then added. Included in this are people, vehicles, street furniture and street lighting.

Under certain circumstances building models can be combined with garden models. In such cases the two types must be coordinated and integrated to form a single model.

Conceptual model

Using an accurate yet easily modified site model, the ground, position of paths, and space formation should be represented as simply as possible.

Various spatial relationships and viewing positions may be explored whilst prominent details such as memorials, fountains, towers, groups of trees or single trees, escarpments and stone blocks can be set in relationship to each other. They can either be made from plastic materials or represented by ready-made objects (Section 3.1.9). Topographic details can easily be integrated with any buildings present. The necessary background information, apart from sketches, is given by topographic plans, and photographs of the original state of the development area.

9 Landscape model as conceptual model. Representation of landscape using miscellaneous items. (*top*)

10 Landscape model as work model, 1:500. Base plate: chipboard; site construction from grey cardboard (full layers); trees: paper balls. Landscape area, tree clusters and the overall concept are all shown, using quite simple means. (*middle*)

11 Landscape model as exhibition model, 1:100. Corrugated cardboard, solid wood, Iceland moss. (*bottom*)

Work model

This gives more detailed information regarding the nature of plants used, and the surface treatment of the traffic, green, and water areas. It includes a detailed representation of the building structures and the way they fit into the surroundings. It is still possible to modify the model. Individual buildings, and single objects such as fountains, statues, etc can easily be moved around. The positions of the planted areas can be changed at will. Different materials may be inserted to judge their surface and colour effects.

12   Garden model as an exhibition model, 1:100. Base plate: 10 mm chipboard. Site: Plaster of Paris, stippled white with emulsion paint. Furniture: balsa-wood, painted white. Green areas: garden weeds. (*top*)

13   Garden model as work model, 1:200. Base plate: 10 mm chipboard. Site: 1.5 mm cardboard; site modulation: 'Plasticine'; buildings: lime tree wood; green areas: Iceland moss; railings: soldered wire. Such a model enables the ground contours and their characteristic shapes to be examined. (*middle*)

14   Garden model as exhibition model, 1:100. Base plate: 13 mm sandwiched timber slabs; site and existing buildings: grey cardboard. Façade sections and arcades are cut out; the free space is a public garden. Trees and bushes: round rods and wooden balls. Ground modelled with grey cardboard, sloped areas. (*below*)

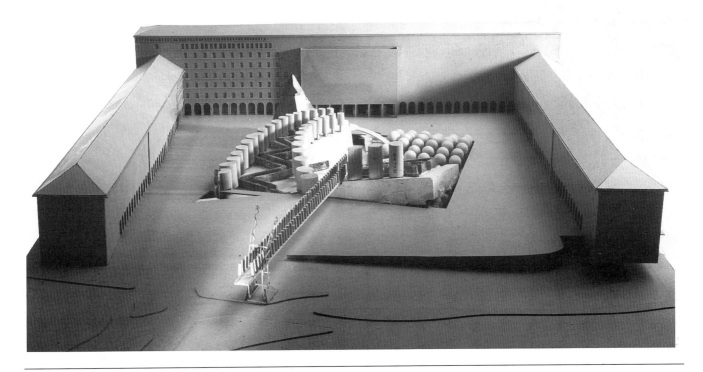

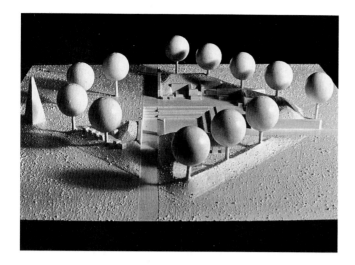

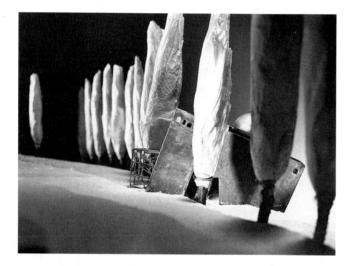

Exhibition model

Planted areas should be positioned for maximum visual effect. The surfaces and features of the garden are represented using suitable materials. The building is shown in detail, demonstrating the way it fits in and relates to its surroundings. The exhibition model cannot be modified, and shows the final stage of the design.

2.2 Building models

Structural models can be subdivided into the following types: urban models, building models, structural models, internal room models and detailed models. The common requirement of each type of model is to represent the spatial, shape and constructional qualities of the project. The following particular aspects are dealt with: how the projected building fits into its surroundings – this means its integration into the prepared site model, which includes topographic details such as profile, site surface and planted areas (see above); the existing buildings against which the projected building has to be erected – the external appearance of the new building must be considered in the context of traffic and neighbourhood arrangements, as well as of existing buildings. When the building structural model is made, emphasis can be laid on any of the following: external appearance, how well it fits in, functional design and details of construction.

The following aspects are of importance for the model:

Shape
1 Overall shape and positioning of the building structure
2 Shape, size and order of spaces
3 Light and direction of light
4 Materials, surfaces and colours
5 Outlook and aesthetic relationship with surroundings

15 Garden model as exhibition model, 1:200. Base plate: 13 mm sandwiched timber slab. Site built from cardboard, stippled with white emulsion paint, and mixed with sand. Trees: wooden balls on round dowels, sprayed white. (*top*)

16 Site made from expanded polystyrene, with layers of gypsum applied by spatula, and stippled white with emulsion paint. Buildings made from steel sheeting; soldered fencing structure. Trees: tissue paper on wooden dowels. (*middle*)

17 Conceptual town model, 1:500. Expanded polystyrene items cut by means of a thermal-saw. (*bottom*)

Function
1 The way building structures and spaces are arranged
2 External and internal enclosures
3 Utilization

Construction
Finally, it is possible to subdivide such models into urban and building structure models on the basis of scale. Urban models usually have scales within the range of 1:1000 to 1:500, and in rare cases 1:200. In such cases, groups of buildings and the various ancillary structures between them are bulked together, as are spaces in between and other similar objects. The building structure model, in contrast, deals solely with the actual building. Depending upon what is needed, it examines its constructional, functional and shape functions. The scale chosen decides whether the building is represented either in its totality, or in sections.

2.2.1 Urban models

Fundamentally, urban models are made on the basis of topographic models. Urban models can be used either as overall city plans (scales: 1:1000 to 1:500), or to represent more detailed sectional plans (scales: 1:500 to 1:200). Within the field of town planning, when problems of squares, roads, rights of way etc. are dealt with, the need may arise for urban models with a larger scale than this (1:100 to 1:50). On the other hand, when overall regional and supra-regional planning is carried out, to find answers to a variety of questions, smaller scales than 1:1000 are also used, i.e. down to 1:2500.

Conceptual model
The task of the urban conceptual model is to give an initial impression of the nature of new buildings in a town or city. It indicates how the buildings are to be distributed and grouped together, and how the whole development will look. By using a topographic model it becomes possible to use easily-shaped materials, ready-made models, and toys to test different modifications of overall planning from the spatial and functional point of view.

18   Town model as exhibition model, 1:500. Base plate: 13 mm sandwiched timber slab. Site made from white cardboard. Buildings from white cardboard. Trees: coloured paper on nails.

Work model

The work model shows us the prevailing conditions. This is of exhibition quality and cannot be altered. However, it is possible to try out different layouts with components which have yet to be designed. Planned buildings may already be in the form of distinct and final entities. Alternative ones can be substituted if so desired.

Exhibition model

This shows precisely how the projected building or buildings fit into the existing landscape and are integrated with the old building stock.

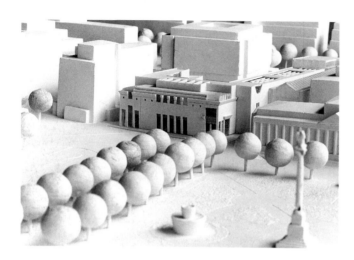

19   Urban work model, 1:500. Base plate: 10 mm chipboard. Layers built up from sandwiched EPS; buildings: solid timber; trees: steel wool. As the site is built up from full layers, it can be altered at any time. (*top*)

20   Urban exhibition model, 1:500. The design is fitted into a Plaster of Paris model supplied by the authority running the competititive tender. Building: methacrylate; façades: polystyrene; trees: paper balls. (*middle*)

21   Urban model, 1:200. Base plate: 19 mm sandwiched timber slab measuring 150×85 cm. Site: cardboard in full layers. Building: methacrylate loadbearing model, clad on the back with coloured paper. Window partitions etched in. Perforated façades: 1 mm glued-on polystyrene; green areas: sprayed grey; roads: white; tree trunks: twisted wires; tree tops: plastic foam used for filters. (*below*)

2.2.2 Building models

Building models with a scale of between 1:500 and 1:200, as needed, are added to either urban or topographic models. A scale of 1:200 is used when a more detailed examination is needed. If scales between 1:200 and 1:50 are employed, the model only shows the building itself, without its surroundings.

Building models show the various components of the façades and roof sections, the shape of the building structure and how joints are made. They also indicate, how the buildings fits in with the site and any existing buildings. Transparent, complete or partial façade areas may be used, so that inspection of the appropriate rooms behind them can take place. Roof and façade areas can also be constructed so that they can be lifted up in order to look at interior design features. Finally, it is possible to dismantle the entire model in order to study the internal space arrangement and distribution.

Conceptual model

A conceptual model can be constructed using simple means and easily-worked materials to show the overall shape and spatial effect. Contrasts are included in shape, size, direction, position, light/dark contrast, colour and surface treatment. Essential features are spontaneity, and flexibility when changes are required.

Work model

Using the work model, one can investigate the shape and spatial relationships of the design details, without having to make any final decisions about the nature of the project. The same applies to constructional and organizational questions which are to be resolved using the work model. It enables one to develop and test relationships with any existing buildings and the surrounding land.

The shape of the rooms, and the way they are arranged, can be visualized more clearly. The internal and external borders and their interplay can be optimized on the model, or perhaps on several variants of the model. While the conceptual model deals mainly with the overall external shape, the work model helps to finalize the nature of the façades and roof. Openings, constructional elements, changes in depth, variations in line of façade and roof are marked, and proportions are investigated. If the material has been selected properly and the work carried out sufficiently well, the work model can then be used as an exhibition model.

Exhibition model

Exhibition models show the final design of the building. They are normally made for presentation purposes, namely competitive tendering, scholastic designs, and for either public or private decision making bodies. They show the exact topographic boundary conditions, and the designs of the building itself, together with such scale impression-forming items as cars, urban features and people. These also serve to emphasize the correct urban context of the new structure.

22   Building model, 1:200. Site cast in concrete. Buildings made from steel sheeting.

23   Building model, 1:50. Site as inclined plane of sandwiched EPS, building: main structure sandwiched EPS; façades: 1 mm polystyrene; windows: methacrylate sheeting, 'Tetraline'; railings: wire.

2.2.3 Structural models

These models show the structural design of a building, without displaying the total external shape. Such models may demonstrate the utilization and jointing techniques, but are usually employed to show the method of construction. Using structural models it is often possible to find solutions to functional and assembly problems.

Constructional problems involving dimensions are frequently solved with the help of such models, by demonstrating them to other people, such as specialist engineers, working on the project. Structural models are usually made on the base of a site model, in the same way as building models. Frequently, certain topographic conditions may have a direct bearing upon the way the structure is designed. Such models are made in scales between 1:200 and 1:50.

Conceptual model
Conceptual models are made from immediately available materials, which can be easily shaped and jointed. Ready-made items, originally intended for a completely different purpose, are often used. They represent the original thoughts of the designer regarding isolated problems of construction, connection and utilization. Often the originator of the design can thus visualize complicated space relationships, or demonstrate them to others.

Work model
While work models should ideally be fully capable of being modified, structural work models often represent the final stage of the project. Individual items and problems affecting details can be worked out and explained to others who are also involved with the project. Provided they are sufficiently well-made, work models can usually also be used for presentation purposes.

Exhibition model
Structural models which have been carefully made are used almost exclusively for presentation and information purposes. Such models are employed by official bodies for information, and also by industry at exhibitions for documentation and publicity purposes.

24 Building model, 1:200. Base plate: grey cardboard with stiffened ribs. Traffic and green areas, open-air theatre: grey cardboard, methacrylate sheeting; lattice structure: soldered wire; trees: steel wool. (*top*)

25 Conceptual model of a staircase, 1:200. Base plate: chipboard; stair treads: balsa-wood. (*bottom*)

2.2.4 Internal room models

Such models represent either single rooms or several rooms at a time. Internal room elements with scales between 1:100 and 1:20 have the job of visualizing spatial, functional and optical questions. Frequently, colours, materials and furniture are selected or designed on the basis of internal room models. They are particularly useful for very important and prominent spaces, such as entrance halls and foyers, staircases, churches and assembly halls.

Important examples of internal room models are those used for designing theatre stages. Internal room models are also widely used for testing paint and material samples.

Conceptual model

Conceptual models of internal rooms are made in order to simulate in the easiest way how space within the room should be allocated. Material which is immediately available is used, often mounted as a kind of stage set. Yet such a system can usually make internal room conditions reasonably comprehensible.

Work model

Design ideas can be clarified and space allocated by using a work model. Decisions are made at this stage, regarding materials, furniture, decoration and lighting. These may, however, be modified at a later stage. Models of theatre stages at this point of development are already prototypes for work to be carried out in the workshops.

Exhibition model

Exhibition models of internal rooms are made in order to present the final design. These models are usually

26 Base plate: chipboard; lattice structure: soldered wire; buildings: balsa-wood; other areas: painted polystyrene, balsa, methacrylate sheeting.

27 Construction model, 1:33. Base plate: sandwiched timber. Frame: poplar wood.

the basis of detailed furnishing of the rooms concerned, in consultation with the interior decorator and the developer. They are widely used when furnishing hospitals, hotels and restaurants, and for installing seating in theatres, concert halls and lecture theatres.

2.2.5 Models of detailed items

Especially complicated single objects, as well as series items that occur over and over again, can be represented and designed with the help of sectional models and models of detailed items. These items may be of a constructional nature, or they can be merely decorative. The scale used varies between 1:10 and 1:1.

Decisions made on the basis of such models usually concern shape, material, surfaces, colour and junctions. Sectional models and detailed item models are usually based upon accurate technical drawings and well-developed design concepts. For this reason therefore,

---

28   Staircase, 1:20 work model. Base plate: chipboard. Treads and wall panels: sandwiched EPS and card. (*left*)

29   Stage set, 1:10. Painted grey cardboard, wooden staves. (*below*)

30   Internal room model, 1:10. Hospital ward. Wall units and façade elements of sandwiched EPS. Furniture: polystyrene, plywood, rigid foamed plastic. (*right*)

31 Model of details, 1:1. Casting knots as pressure dowel connection. Painted lime wood, plywood, round timber.

32 Furniture model, 1:15. High chest of drawers. Painted maple wood. (*below left*)

33 Façade model, 1:10. Loadbearing model: 10 mm plywood sheeting. Areas from mahogany veneer, all profiles made from pear wood, stained black and polished; windows from methacrylate; mullions and transoms from glued on solid timber. (*below right*)

no conceptual or work models are usually made, only exhibition models.

Exhibition models

Models of details are made at this stage of the work to examine alternative ways of solving constructional or other problems. In addition, detailed models are used for colour and material studies, and configurational problems. Very detailed models of sections of a building are made when solving queries involving junctions, sections of spaces and façades, decoration and ornamentation.

2.3 Special models

This group mainly comprises models of special objects, furnishing and designs. Scales used vary between 1:10 and 1:1. Although these models are usually made as prototypes at the first stage of design, there is little difference in quality between them and the final exhibition model.

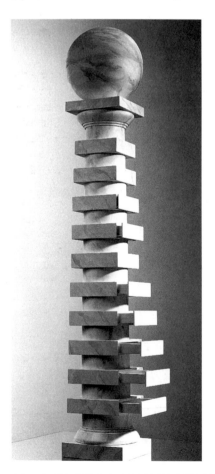

3 Materials and Tools

Numerous different materials are used for making architectural models, both in the basic structure, and for additional items to be added afterwards. The choice depends upon the stage of development of the design, the basic idea behind it, and the surface upon which everything is mounted. The scale of the model, the tools available and the manual skills of the person making the model are also important criteria. The deciding factor is probably, above all, personal preference together with a knowledge of the effect which may be produced by the use of different materials.

It is quite wrong to consider that it does not matter which carton is used with which paper, or the type of wood that is employed in conjunction with a specific metal. It is always necessary to look at the visual effect of the material and the way it is worked. Beginners, in particular, must gather together as comprehensive a collection of materials as possible, and augment it continuously. Ready-made items, i.e. special pre-fabricated objects, originally intended for quite different purposes, can often be added to the model to produce quite surprising effects. It is wise to be continuously on the lookout for such items. All these objects should be stocked within easy reach of the work bench. They stimulate the imagination and make it possible to produce original but correct structural entities.

For the same reason it is a good idea to examine carefully, well-made and attractive models constructed by other people. One should look at the reasons behind the selection of specific materials and the techniques adopted, and compare the effects achieved with those intended. At first it is likely that one may merely copy other people's methods. However, as one's own knowledge and ability increase, a more individual and personal model-building technique evolves. It is always necessary to consider the ultimate purpose of the model. Even if the model possesses its own reality with its own artistic effect, this is not really the final aim.

All the materials used for model-making require specific tools. These range from scissors for cutting paper to a lathe for modelling wood. Whatever the tool acquired, it is always worthwhile buying good quality equipment. Only sharp cutters produce exact edges. Good tools give long service, but must be cared for, sharpened, oiled, and generally maintained.

34 Tools for working with paper and cardboard. Steel setsquare, ruler, pencils, tracing wheel, gouge needle, needles, polishing steel, universal knife, scissors, adhesives.

When dealing with sharp objects and, particularly, fast-running machines it is imperative to constantly be aware of the danger of injuries. It is not just the danger of getting one's fingers chopped off. Even the smallest drop of blood can ruin a model, while a sticking-plaster on one's finger makes it difficult to continue working. Beginners sometimes underrate the tools and machines used for model-making. Because they are smaller, they appear to be less dangerous than the large machines used in carpentry workshops. Wearing safety glasses or breathing masks may be inconvenient, but a splinter in one's eye can cause permanent damage, and dust from grinding machines irritates eyes and air passages, often causing asthma. Solvent vapours can impair your health, and many are explosive. Therefore, ventilate the room well and do not smoke. The hardeners in two-component adhesives may attack the skin. Use thin rubber gloves to protect your hands.

Always practise handling an unfamiliar material before using it on your model. When you have gained some experience in the use of established materials, you will soon become adept in extending your skills to new materials of a similar nature. The same applies where new tools and machines are concerned. Colour tests should be carried out on all paints used. Adequate quantities of self-mixed paints should be retained to enable the same shade to the applied to later modifications or sections which have been repaired after damage. Water-soluble paints dry to a lighter shade than when they are applied, while oil paints and lacquers are darker when dry. For model-making purposes it makes more sense to keep small quantities in tubes or small pots, rather than storing them in large tins, where they easily set solid.

3.1 Materials

The materials which are most widely used for model-building can be subdivided into 11 different groups:

3.1.1 Paper, carton, cardboard

Such materials are excellent for use at all stages of the development work (conceptual models, work models and exhibition models). They are readily available, there is a wide choice, they are cheap and easy to work and to modify. In general, it is essential to consider the specific properties of all these materials, as described below. The materials will only be used at their best if these criteria are observed.

Sizes
Sheets are usually either 70×100 cm or 61×86 cm in size. Smaller sizes can be obtained by halving the large sheets, down to DIN A4 (210×294 mm). In addition to these standard sizes, certain special sizes are also made.

35 Micro-corrugated cardboard, corrugated cardboard, Finnish cardboard, cork, soft fibre board, lined EPS, grey cardboard. (*left*)

36 Three-dimensional shape made from carton. (*below*)

37 Façade design, 1:50. Conceptual design. Grey cardboard, drawing carton, drawing in Indian ink. (*above*)

38 Building model: exhibition model, 1:200. Methacrylate sheeting, window sections scored in. Polystyrene sheets and round rods. (*below*)

Direction of grain

In the case of all machine-made papers, the fine paper fibres tend to lie in the direction in which the material has run through the machine. The direction in line with the grain is therefore somewhat stiffer than when perpendicular to it. Folds which run parallel to the direction of the grain are smoother. Pleats taken across the grain direction, particularly with thicker paper, often tear. Just like wood, it is easier to work paper across the grain direction than along it. Wet paper becomes wavy and does not smooth out again even when it dries. This has to be considered when applying glues and paints. Nitrobenzene, methylated spirits and similar solvents do not cause paper to swell up in the same way as water.

Mass per unit area

Paper is classified in the trade by its mass per square metre. For example, thin copy paper weighs 25 g/m², typewriter paper 80 g/m², and the paper used for this book 130 g/m². If the weight of the paper is more than 180 g/m² it is called carton. A sheet of DIN A4 paper has an area of 1/16 m². To find out the mass per unit area, 16 such sheets are placed onto a scale, and the weight is recorded. Cardboard is classified according to thickness (see below).

Lignin content – yellowing

When paper is made, the raw material, wood, must be separated into very thin cellulose fibres. This is carried out either mechanically by grinders or, rather more expensively, by chemical means which separate cellulose from lignin. The higher the cellulose content of the paper, the stronger it is and the less likely it will be to yellow in sunlight. Paper and carton are called 'lignin-free', when they are free from ground-up lignin particles. Other types have either a 'low lignin content' or a 'high lignin content'.

Sizing

Paper itself is porous (blotting paper). To prevent printer's ink, Indian ink and normal ink from running, certain materials are added to paper and carton during manufacture which are called sizes. Strongly-sized papers are particularly stable for use with inks. With transparent tracing papers Indian ink remains on the surface and can be scraped off, whereas normal ink penetrates somewhat further.

Main types of paper and carton

Typewriter paper

Usually 80 g/m². Sold in packets of 500 sheets DIN A4, and available in different quality standards. For model-building use well-sized, lignin-free paper, with a density of not less than 80 g/m².

Layout and marker paper

Light copy paper is available in rolls. (For example: 25 g/m², 30 cm wide and 200 m² long – weight 1.5 kg)

Drawing paper (150 and 175 g/m²)

Drawing carton (200, 250 and 300 g/m²)

Lignin-free, white, usually heavily-sized. The surface is smooth, rough or extra smooth. Mainly available in sheets (about 70×100 cm) or half sheets (50×70 cm), or alternatively, 61×86 cm (half-sheets measure 43×61 cm). Thicker drawing cartons than this are also available, but these are sold according to thickness. Single thickness equals 0.5 mm, full thickness approximately 1.5 mm and double thickness approximately 3 mm. Extremely thin aluminium and plastic foils which are incorporated ensure that carton retains an accurate dimensional stability. Thick drawing carton can be cut very accurately and is easy to glue. All types of paints can be easily applied by brush or spray-gun.

Cardboard

The difference between this and carton is its colour. It can either be grey, because it contains residues of printed recycled paper, or brown due to its content of boiled and ground woodpulp particles. Grey paper is the usual cardboard used by bookbinders. It is tough and can be bent easily. It can only be cut with a knife that is run along a ruler. Brown 'leather cardboard' is even tougher. Brown machine woodpulp cardboard and lighter 'straw cardboard' are more brittle, looser, and can be cut freehand with a knife. This material is to be preferred when fabricating site models.

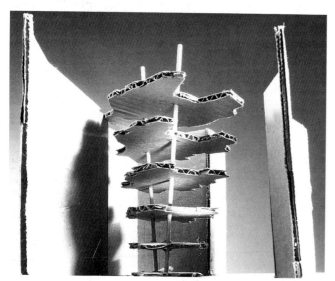

39 Group of trees, 1:20. Corrugated cardboard, wooden rods.

Normal standard sizes are 70×100 cm, and 75×100 cm, as well as smaller dimensions. Cardboard is purchased according to its thickness. There are several different thicknesses on the market, varying between 0.5 mm and 4.0 mm. A common type is machine woodpulp cardboard at either 1.05 mm or 2.5 mm thick.

Foam plastic cardboard

This material is sold under different proprietary names. It is very light, yet extremely rigid because it contains a core of foamed plastic that is covered on both sides by paper. It can be cut easily with a knife. The cover paper yellows and must therefore be glued over with lignin-free paper, painted, or covered in some other way. Before glues are applied to the exposed foam plastic, it is necessary to carry out some tests to see whether the solvent in the glue is compatible with the plastic material. If the material is cut, the exposed foam plastic will be visible at the edges and will remain so, even when painted. It is best to cover the exposed core with paper. Usual sizes: 70×100 cm and 140×100 cm. Thicknesses are 3 mm, 5 mm and 10 mm.

Corrugated cardboard

This material is available in a wide variety of qualities and sizes. The corrugated section can either be on one side only, or on both sides, sandwiched by smooth paper. Accordingly, it may either be rolled up or lie stiff. There are also thicker slabs containing several layers of cor-

40   Internal room model, 1:10. Base plate: chipboard, wall panels: 'Chromo' substitute carton on expanded polystyrene. Total size: 160×70 cm.

41   Different grades of foamed plastics.

42 Building model, 1:200. Base plate: chipboard; site: glued paper; building: expanded polystyrene.

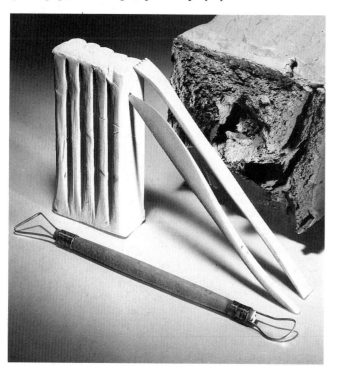

43 'Plasticine' and clay. Various modelling tools.

rugation. It is a good material for site models because it is so light. However, if it is subject to excessive loading it becomes compressed. The finer the corrugations, the more rigid the material is likely to prove.

Cork sheeting

This is on the market in various colours, degrees of graining and thicknesses in do-it-yourself stores, and in shops which sell floor and wall cladding. The sheeting is available in sizes of up to 100×150 cm, or in the form of rolls. The thickness varies between 1 mm and 5 mm. It is necessary to look at the structure of cork sheeting. If the cork has been insufficiently ground, graining can adversely affect the dimensional stability. Cork sheeting used in engineering (seals in the car industry) or in medicine is particularly suitable for our purposes.

Apart from the sheeting mentioned here, there are a number of other, similar materials which are suitable for model-building because of their colour, ease of use and strength. Examples are bituminous felt and wood-fibre cardboard.

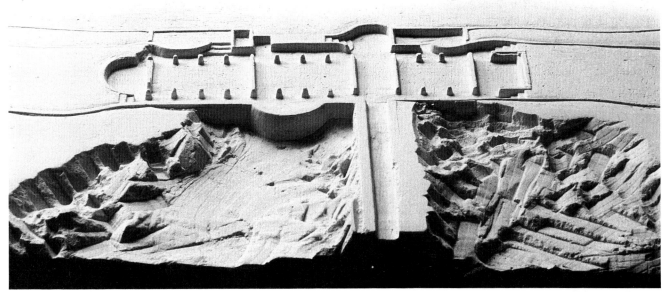

44 Building model, 1:100. Entry level cut from block of Plaster of Paris.

45 Garden model, 1:50. Subconstruction: plywood; site modelled from gypsum. Reinforcement: wire netting.

3.1.2 Foamed plastics

The most common of all of these is expanded polystyrene, which is marketed under a number of different trade names. Foamed plastics are widely used. Shapes and surfaces can be cut from them, particularly for conceptual and work models for town planning exercises, or when the need for special design models arises. Expanded or extruded polystyrene foams can be easily cut with a knife or by using a hot wire (thermal-saw). The objects can then be finished off using a file and sandpaper. Other plastic foams, such as phenolics and PVC cannot be cut with a hot wire but only by means of a metal saw or, when very thin, using a knife. They are so rigid that they can be planed, drilled, put into a lathe or sanded. It is essential to wear a breathing mask as protection against the sanding dust. Toxic vapours are emitted when these materials are heated.

It is always necessary to use the correct glues when jointing plastic foams, because an incorrect solvent may make holes. It is best to experiment with the glue first. Surfaces can be painted or sprayed with any water-soluble paints, such as distemper and acrylics. If synthetic resins or nitro-cellulose paints are used, the surface must be pre-treated with a water-soluble coating, which is then sanded down to provide a smooth base.

Expanded polystyrene (EPS) is made in slabs measuring 50×100 cm. The thickness varies between 10 mm and 100 mm. Other plastic foams are sold in sizes of 125×62.5 cm, and have a thickness of between 1 and 3 mm, or 250×125 cm, having a thickness of between 4 and 65 mm.

46   Stage set, 1:10. Substructure: expanded polystyrene, gypsum applied by spatula. Perforated steel sheeting; fencing made from soldered wire.

47   Conceptual model, 1:500. Base plate: 8 mm plywood; building and trees: 'Plasticine'.

3.1.3 Modelling materials

Gypsum

Gypsum (Plaster of Paris) is needed by the designer either for correcting or amending existing gypsum models, or for building free site shapes and special objects. Casting entire models in gypsum is a specialized job (see page 72 onwards). It is, however, necessary to learn how to use gypsum, in order to modify site conditions in a model. Roads and footpaths need to be marked, and the model of the building must be correctly positioned. For our purposes we use white ground alabaster gypsum. To make it up, gypsum is sprinkled into water until it has absorbed nearly all the moisture. The mass is then stirred for two minutes and used immediately. When the gypsum starts to set, it cannot be re-liquified by adding more water, as the half-set gypsum merely starts to crumble. It is necessary to make a fresh mixture. If cellulose glue is added, the setting process is retarded. Gypsum powder can only be kept for a limited time because it absorbs moisture from the air and cannot be properly hardened after exposure. Various other proprietary modelling masses set more slowly than gypsum.

Note: Dry gypsum absorbs moisture from a freshly applied gypsum slurry so rapidly that the new layer sets immediately. If one wishes to carry out further work on a gypsum casting, the existing gypsum mass must be saturated with water using a brush or sponge. Using a knife or chisel, the gypsum can be removed without breaking the entire model. When a gypsum

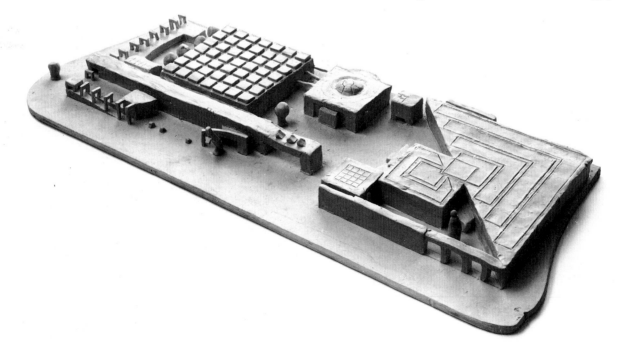

48 Stage set, 1:50. Base plate: 19 mm sandwiched timber slab; structure modelled from clay. (*above*)

49 Building and garden model, 1:100. Base plate: sandwiched timber slab. Site made from clay and straw. Building constructed from soldered brass profiles. Fence from solid timber. (*below*)

model is dry, it can be sawn, drilled, filed, and so on. The gypsum must be moistened whenever new layers are applied.

'Polyfilla'

This is a white powder which hardens much more slowly than gypsum. It is used for repairs and alterations. In contrast to gypsum, the material shrinks slightly when it dries.

Clay and 'Plasticine'

Clay and 'Plasticine' (a mix of waxes, pigments and fillers) are two easily-shaped kinds of plastic masses, which can be readily worked and re-shaped. They are used in conceptual and work models to indicate shapes. Clay stocks and clay models must be protected from drying-out using plastic foil.

3.1.4 Wood

Apart from paper and cardboard, solid timber and timber products are the most usual materials employed for architectural models. From the base plate down to the most minute details the properties of rigidity, dimensional accuracy and ease of fabrication make wood one of the most valuable raw materials available.

Solid timber

This shows its natural colour and graining. Major structural properties of timber, such as the annual rings, knots and fissures, could give problems and may affect the scalar properties of the model. Optically inactive woods are better for our purposes than timbers with prominent features. Building blocks are often made from timber and painted afterwards. Lighter types of wood are therefore to be preferred. It is also much easier to distinguish profiles and shape details, as well as differences in levels, on white or lightly-coloured objects. If dark objects are used, small, shadowed sections can easily be lost.

When working with wood, hardness and direction of grain are the most important features. Balsa-wood can easily be cut with a knife, but is somewhat porous and cannot withstand much weight. Hardwoods, such as maple, pear and alder, must be sawn, but when sanded down, exhibit smooth and homogenous surfaces. In between are the softwoods, such as lime, poplar and fir. The colours range from yellowish/white (poplar and maple) to yellowish (lime or abachi), reddish (pear or

50 Structural model, 1:10. Solid timber. Height about 150 cm. (*left*)

51 Timber materials: plywood (glued veneers); aircraft plywood; chipboard; sandwiched timber slab; hard fibre plate (hardboard). (*below*)

alder) right down to reddish-brown (mahogany). All timbers yellow in the sun. This is more obvious with pale woods than with dark ones.

Solid timber can be bought in timber stores, do-it-yourself shops, and in the form of offcuts from carpentry workshops. It is best to get the pieces and laths pre-cut, which can then be worked further without requiring excessive effort. Hardware shops stock finished timber profiles such as dowelling, wooden balls and so on.

Timber products
These are mainly used as base panels. Apart from rigidity, it is necessary to consider their weight per unit area. Chipboard and hard fibreboard are denser and heavier than plywood units with hollow cores.

Veneered panels
These are available in thicknesses of between 13 and 45 mm. The length goes up to 183 cm and the width up to 510 cm. The central core consists of wooden staves, which are closely set side-by-side, the whole being sandwiched between outside veneer layers.

Plywood
This consists of wood veneers, which are glued crosswise over each other. The thickness of each layer varies between 0.2 and 6 mm. Aircraft plywood is made in 0.4, 0.6, 0.8 and 1 mm thicknesses. Normal plywood, however, goes up to 15 mm in thickness. Lengths of plywood sheets, up to 303 cm, with widths of 122 cm and 152.5 cm, are on the market. The veneers are similar to those used by joiners, and are commonly made from abachi, beech, birch, limba, makore, and other timbers.

Particle board
Timber particles, which are held together by synthetic resins, go under the name of particle board. The soft fibre boards are more loosely bound, and in consequence have less than half the density of the hardboard sheets (densities 0.23–0.4 kg/dm³ as against 0.95 kg/dm³). The hardboard sheets have thicknesses of betweeen 2.5 mm and 6 mm. Sizes go up to 200×600 cm.

Chipboard
This consists of glued-together wood chips and is rather dense. It is easier to handle in panels, which have a low-density central core. Thicknesses vary between 6 and 30 mm. The size of the panels varies according to the manufacturer. The normal maximum is 180×510 cm.

52 Solid timber.

53 Town planning model, 1:500. Base plate: chipboard veneered with aircraft plywood; building: poplar timber.

54 Building model, 1:100. Base plate: chipboard; site: cork; square made from thin facing timber sheeting; buildings: fir. Trees made from twisted wires. The wooden structure is fitted on as a complete entity. (*above*)

55 Building model: exhibition model, 1:200. Base plate chipboard, covered with black tissue paper. Building and all separate parts: massive pear timber. (*below*)

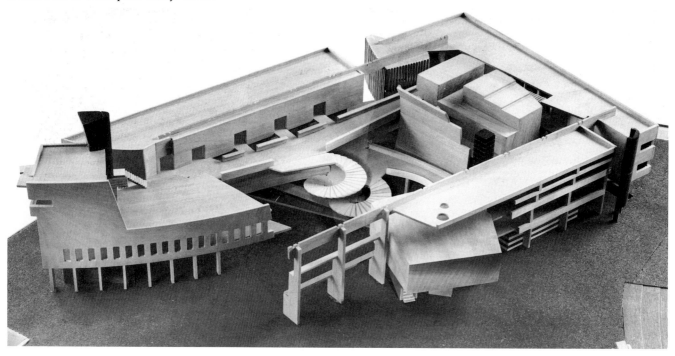

3.1.5 Glass

Mineral glass (window glass)
This is hard and brittle, and is seldom used for model construction. It is necessary to use a glass cutter (diamond or hardened steel wheel) to cut a groove along the edge of a ruler. A diamond gives the best results, but the hardened steel wheel is more robust. Do not press too hard, but use a firm and steady pressure. Moisten the groove and hammer gently from the underside. A pane which has its groove on its top side is placed against an exact and sharp edge and pressed downwards.

When narrow strips are to be broken off, the pane should be supported between wooden laths. Any slivers adhering to the pane should be dislodged with an old file, otherwise there is a danger of injuries occurring. Edges which are not straight must be ground down by an expert. Window glass is about 1.8 mm in thickness, while plate glass is normally 3–4 mm or more in thickness.

3.1.6 Methacrylate sheeting, polystyrene

Methacrylate sheeting
This bears the chemical name of poly-methyl-methacrylate, and is sold under a variety of trade names ('Plexiglas', 'Perspex', etc.). It is a synthetic material, light in weight, elastic, and much easier to cut than mineral glass. In contrast to normal glass, it is easily scratched. This is the reason why it is delivered wrapped in protective paper. This material is available in numerous varieties – glass-clear, translucent and opaque, in many colours and different surface structures, i.e. smooth, grained, grooved, etc.

Methacrylates can be supplied in two different quality standards, depending upon the way they are made. Extruded methacrylate glass (thickness 1.5–8 mm) can contain streaks and may smear when planed. It is reasonably good for our purposes. The cast version (0.8–250 mm in thickness) is more expensive, but the glass is clear and easier to work with.

Polystyrene
This is white or grey, with other colours also available on request. It is similar to the methacrylates, but not transparent. Thickness is between 0.5 and 10 mm, and sheet dimensions are up to 200×100 cm.

If façades, grassed areas and water surfaces are to be represented, foils and sheets of either of these two materials are quite excellent. If the material is up to 3 mm thick, it can be cut relatively easily by means of a modelling knife. A ruler is laid along the appropriate

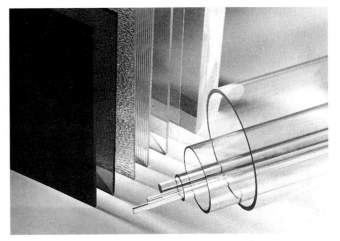

56   Methacrylate sheeting, tubes and rods.

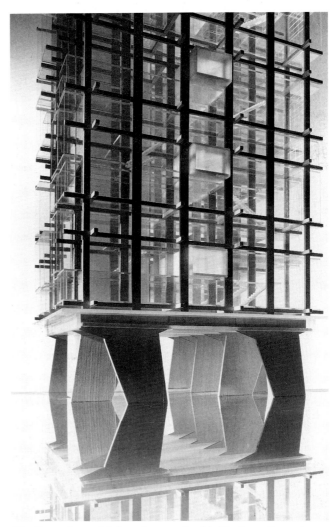

57   Base plate: chipboard, coated with black methacrylate sheeting. Construction: maple timber. Attached building elements: transparent methacrylate sheeting. Ancillary elements: opaque methacrylate.

edge, and a deep cut is made with a hooked knife blade. This cut is then enlarged with a normal knife blade and broken by placing it over an exact edge and applying pressure. Apart from this, the material can be sawn, drilled, milled, turned, ground and polished. Care must be taken regarding heating-up which occurs when the material is worked. The cut must not get too warm otherwise it starts to streak. Protective spectacles must be worn if any machine is employed for working & with the material. When the material gets hot it will soften, making it possible to use a hot-air device to bend thinner sheets. Do not forget to remove protective paper before carrying out such an operation. Because of its thermo-plastic nature the material can also be extruded. This is a technique which requires special equipment and is used only rarely in connection with architectural models.

Special adhesives may be used to join acrylic materials together. Unless the recommended proprietary adhesives are employed, it is advisable to try out the

58   Building model, 1:50. Base plate: chipboard, covered with carton. Wall and floor areas: polystyrene and methacrylate; windows: methacrylate; partitions: 'Letraline'; railings: wire. The model can be taken apart. (*above*)

59   Building model, 1:200. Base plate: 19 mm sandwich timber, covered with polystyrene, plate structure etched. Building – walls and ceilings: polystyrene; windows and skylights: 0.8 mm methacrylate foil; fencing: soldered wires. Trees: twisted wire with filter foam plastics – white in colour. It is possible to inspect the interior. (*below*)

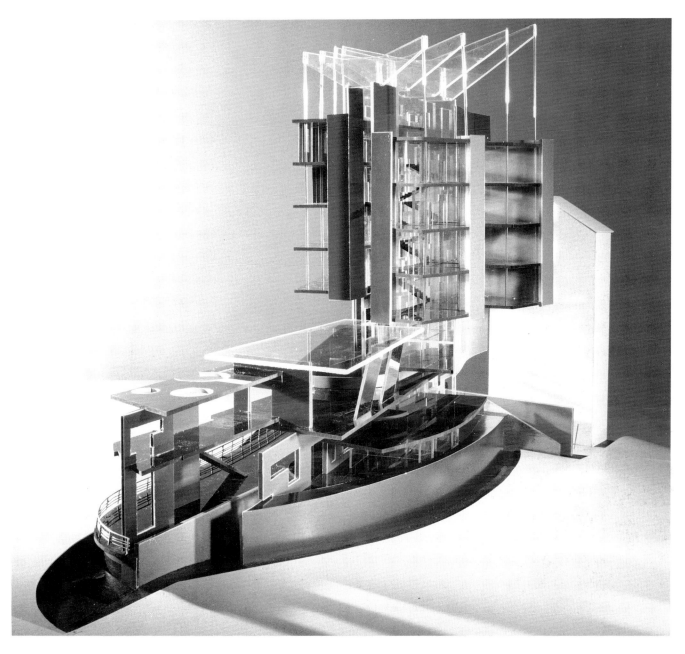

jointing glues first. Screws can also be used. The drilled holes must be large enough to avoid stresses. These can lead to cracks and breakages.

The surface can be scratched, made matt or re-polished. Lines, squares and graphic structures can be scored in with a steel gouge needle, similar to engraving work. If the score marks are untreated they appear white in colour. If desired, one can use a piece of cotton wool or gauze to rub wet paint into the score marks. Allow the paint to dry, and re-polish. In order to provide matt surfaces, masking paper is applied to surfaces which should stay clear, and the surface is then treated with spray adhesive or similar.

60 Building model, 1:100. Base plate: 16 mm chipboard. Fencing: plywood, covered with carton. Building: horizontal and vertical sections made from black and colourless methacrylate sheeting, partially coated with coloured 'Chromo' substitute carton. Railings soldered from straightened wire. Existing buildings: 3 mm sandwiched EPS.

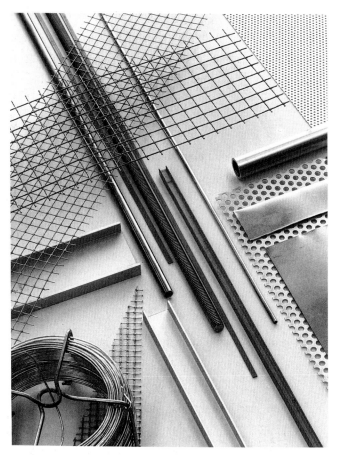

61 Wire, brass profiles, tubes, aluminium profiles, threaded rods, aluminium and brass sheeting. Perforated sheeting and wire netting.

62 Soldered wire structure. Covered with stretched plastic foil.

3.1.7 Metal

The following metal items are incorporated in architectural models: wire, sheet metal, wire netting and profiles. They are mainly used to represent loadbearing structures, steel constructions, façades, railings and other metal parts. In addition, they help to interpret the basic idea behind the design. Base plates, for example, can be made from aluminium, while floors, walls, roof sections, traffic areas and water surfaces can be fabricated from various pieces of sheet metal. Entire structures can be made from coloured metal parts. If a large collection of such components is readily available for use it can provide the incentive to try out some extremely interesting experiments.

Special tools are needed when working with metal. It is necessary to cut precisely and to produce accurate angles. The correct pliers and shears are needed when metal components are being bent or cut. Safety spectacles must always be worn when metal is worked, whether it is sawn, drilled, turned, milled or shaped.

Soldering is used to make lattices, carriers or entire frameworks (further details are given on page 98). Metal sheeting is best attached to other flat surfaces by means of double-sided sticky foil. There is little need to form a particularly strong joint in such a case. Surfaces can be etched or scored, as with methacrylates, and colour rubbed in. Grinding produces a matt surface, and polishing increases the effectiveness of flat surfaces. Brass and copper look particularly effective when coloured chemically. It is necessary to get in touch with specialist firms in order to obtain nickel-plate or chromium-plate metals.

3.1.8 Paint

63 Soldered wire structure. Measurements: approximately 60×15×60 cm.

An alternative to keeping model-building materials in their natural state is to paint them well. Apart from supplying the correct colour, painting also serves to provide a homogenous surface, closes up pores, and hides the true nature of the material used. The same paint acts differently when applied to different surfaces. Always try out the paints first, and make colour-coat samples. Very porous substrata, such as gypsum or soft fibreboard, should always be coated with size in order to close up the pores. Larger timber surfaces should be sanded first with coarse grain sandpaper, and then with very fine emery paper. This process can be repeated several times. If timber is kept in its natural state, dust is less likely to settle on it. Smaller timber items may be sprayed several times with very thin paint, with attention being paid to the correct drying times. Metal parts are first rubbed with acetone or petroleum ether to remove grease. No undercoat is then required. All that is necessary is some very light sanding.

The main paints used are water-soluble emulsion paints. Acrylics are also widely used. Depending upon the surface to be treated, synthetic resin paints and nitro-cellulose lacquers are of importance. Tube caps should be lightly greased with 'Vaseline' to prevent the paint attached to them from drying out. Tins should be closed tightly and stored upside down, to ensure that no air can enter.

Paints are applied in the following ways: using a round or flat paintbrush; stippling with a round stipple brush; employing a paint roller; using a spray-gun.

For environmental protection reasons spray canisters containing fluoro-hydrocarbons should not be used.

3.1.9 Natural and manufactured bits and pieces

Small finished pieces are mainly used to represent plants, trees and bushes, as well as such scale impression-giving items as cars, street lamps and furniture. Small finished pieces can also be used successfully to cover constructional joints. It is necessary to develop a feel for collecting bits together which may be used some time in the future to provide the finishing touches to models. Nature gives us many useful bits and pieces: pine cones and small twigs, dried strands of sheep fleece and fruits of numerous plants. Then there are the fields of electronics, model aircraft, model ships and model railways, all of which are rich sources of suitable items. Wooden balls and dowels can symbolize bushes and

trees. A gasket profile can become a park bench, and an aluminium rivet an overhead lamp.

3.1.10 Very small components

The important very small parts used for model-building include pins, needles, thread, plaited cords, 'Perlon' string, and many other components, particularly those used by anglers. Self-adhesive paper and coloured metal foils in various widths and thicknesses are also widely used. Pins and marker pins are required not only for fixing parts of the model during assembly, but also to represent figures (Chapter 8: Materials Used to Indicate Scale).

Threads are used to indicate rope constructions, and also the boundaries of roads, paths and areas in work models. Fine 'Perlon' or nylon strings, between 0.1 mm and 1 mm thick, as well as plaited cords of all types, are obtainable in shops catering for anglers. Such shops also stock miniature key-rings, and similar items. Shops that sell model aircraft and model ship components usually also stock miniature rope-handling items. Self-adhesive plastic or paper tapes, 0.5 mm wide and upwards, which are made in numerous different colours, can be used to represent window frames, door profiles and framing.

3.1.11 Adhesives, adhesive tape, adhesive sheet

Nowadays it is possible to obtain adhesives which are able to join together virtually any material.

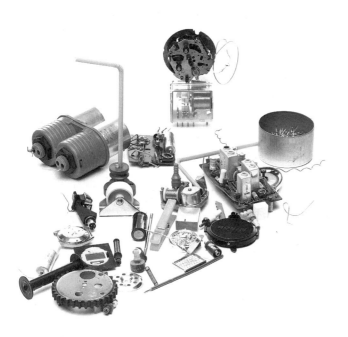

64 Bits and pieces.

65 Conceptual model, 1:100.

However, the following three points must be observed:

- the construction material must be able to withstand the solvent used in the adhesive.
- the glue must suit the shape and size of the surface to be glued.
- the surface to be glued must be properly pre-treated.

The term 'to glue' describes a firm joining of parts by means of a layer of adhesive. This layer is produced by hardening of the adhesive, which may take place either by a drying (woodworker's glue) or by a chemical reaction (two-component adhesive). Apart from the nature of the glued areas, and the pre-treatment used, the strength of the joint is influenced by the following two factors: adhesion and cohesion.

If a wet piece of paper sticks to a glass pane, or two pieces of glass are held together by a layer of water in between, the forces which hold the substances together are known as adhesion forces. Good adhesion is obtained if there is close contact between the material to be glued and the film of adhesive. Such a close contact can only be achieved if there are no air bubbles or foreign particles between the material layer and the layer of adhesive. This means that the contact layers must be clean, and free from grease and dust. If the material surface is roughened slightly, adhesion is improved, because foreign matter is removed and the surface area is enlarged.

Cohesion, on the other hand, describes the way the adhesive particles are held together. Cohesion depends upon the quality of the adhesive. Cohesion forces are maximized when the adhesive film is applied evenly and in a thin layer.

When using different adhesives it is also useful to consider that there are glues which are able to fill small gaps and cracks. Two-component glues, cellulose acetate glues and white woodworker's glues fall into such a category. Super-glues and glues containing solvents, on the other hand, require surfaces which fit very well to each other. Keep the boxes and packaging in which the glues are supplied, because they often contain detailed instructions regarding the way the glues are to be used.

Types of adhesives

White woodworker's glue
This consists of synthetic resin particles, which are suspended in water. After the water has evaporated, the synthetic resin particles form an almost transparent film. One of the requirements for this adhesive is that at least one of the components is porous, so that the solvent water can evaporate. This adhesive is mainly used for joining wood, veneers and cork. It is not particularly advisable to use white adhesive to glue textiles, carton and paper, because the water causes the paper to crinkle up. Use special bookbinder's glue instead.

Glues containing solvents
Such glues consist of either synthetic resins or synthetic rubbers, which form a solution by means of a solvent. As the solvent evaporates, the adhesive film dries. As far as we are concerned, this means that the solvent must be able to escape either through the material or through the glued joint. It is only possible to use such adhesives when the material is somewhat porous (i.e. paper, cardboard, textiles, leather, timber). Alternatively, if such a glue is used with dense materials (metals or plastics), the glued joint must be long and thin.

Note that many materials can be attacked by the solvents used. Even if instructions are supplied by the manufacturers, carry out some gluing tests yourself. For polystyrene, methacrylates, soft and hard PVC, special adhesives are supplied, (acetone and various model glues).

Contact adhesives
Contact adhesives are mainly used in model-building, to glue together the various layers which represent the terrain in topographic models. They are also employed when two materials are to be glued together which do not permit vapours to escape. Basically, both material surfaces should be covered with thin coats of the adhesive. The solvent is then allowed to evaporate. Afterwards the two components are pressed together, briefly and strongly. A rubber hammer, or better still a rubber roller, which unlike a lamb's-wool roller does not leave any loose threads, should be used for such a purpose.

Two-component adhesives
A two-component adhesive consists of a binder and a hardener, which are mixed together prior to use and applied immediately. The mix ratio and the time of working are given in the instructions supplied by the manufacturer. Only mix very little at a time, as some of these adhesives have very short reaction periods (around 5 minutes). The adhesive layer is capable of withstanding very high loading (some such adhesives, when fully set, can withstand up to 300 kg/cm²). Such adhesives are used for joining metals, pieces of ceramics, glass and hard plastics to each other.

Super-glues
Super-glues have an important part to play in model-building. When a rapid and permanent joint is needed, and it is not possible to hold the components or press them together for any length of time, such adhesives are invaluable. They set under the action of light or the

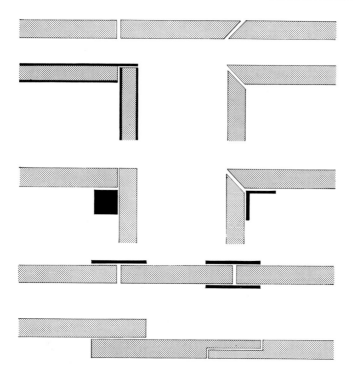

66 Types of glued joints: mitre joint, butt joint, butt joint with cover.

moisture content of the air. There are super-glues for both non-porous materials and porous ones. These glues can be used for metals, rubber, synthetic resins, glass, porcelain or textiles.

When using super-glues take great care that the adhesive does not come into contact with the skin, particularly the eyelids.

Nature of joint to be glued

The strength of a glued joint does not only depend upon the use of the correct adhesive, but also on the nature of the joint. It is important to increase the area which is being glued.

The most important shapes of the joint are the following:

- flat connection
- slanting connection
- flat connection with cover along surface
- flat connection with flap along one side
- flat connection with flaps on both sides
- mitre joint
- simple plate joint
- simple overlap joint

Preparation of surfaces to be joined

1 Clean foreign matter from the surfaces (paint residues, dust, residue of adhesives)
2 Roughen surfaces by sanding
3 Degrease surfaces to be joined (acetone, alcohol, nitro-benzene)
4 Allow surfaces to dry
5 Do not touch prepared surfaces (avoid getting grease from your skin onto them)
6 Apply a thin and even layer of adhesive
7 Wait for the prescribed period of time
8 Avoid getting dirt or dust on to the prepared surfaces. Stop sanding and sawing until the parts have been joined together

Adhesive tapes and adhesive foils

Apart from applying adhesives directly, model-building involves the use of adhesive tapes and double-sided adhesive foil. Adhesive tape is used when parts are to be fixed provisionally. When removing the tape, take care that the material surface is not damaged. Use the weakly adherent adhesive crêpe tapes for such purposes. Adhesive foil is best for sticking paper (coloured and decorated paper) upon carrier materials such as polystyrene, methacrylates, metal sheeting or similar. Such substances can also be joined together by means of double-sided adhesive foils. It is essential that the components treated in such a way should not be porous, and that they should possess good surfaces which must be free from foreign matter, dust and grease. An advantage of such foils is that it becomes possible to join larger areas together, rapidly. Coloured adhesive tapes, 0.5 mm wide or more, are useful for representing window sections in scales of 1:200, 1:100 and 1:50.

Surfaces for cutting materials

Special rubber surfaces are a considerable help when used as a base for cutting up materials. If cardboard or timber is used as a base for cutting there is always the danger that the knife which is led along the ruler may be deflected in its path, or that the base may fall to pieces after it has been used for some time. A homogenous surface, on the other hand, neither deflects not blunts the blade of the cutter. Accurate cuts with clean and sharp edges are produced every time.

3.2 Tools

Whether one starts model-building as a student, or as an architect in an architect's office, a certain minimum number of tools are needed.

All tools used for model-building must be of first-rate quality. As far as we are concerned, so-called combination tools and equipment are of no use. They always represent a compromise.

It is of extreme importance that the tools are well looked after and stored properly. Work on a model can only proceed at a reasonable rate if all tools are kept clearly arranged in a wall cupboard or a proper tool chest. The eight categories listed below do not all have to be acquired at once. A simple set is all that is necessary when starting. Good results can be achieved with such a set, particularly when making conceptual and work models.

Those who see in model-building not only an aid to their work, but also a creative activity, rapidly expand their stock of tools.

Initial set of tools

- 30 cm steel ruler
- 50 cm cutting ruler
- set square
- small and large universal knives with spare blades
- hooked knife for cutting and scoring of methacrylate sheets and thicker plastic sheets
- cutting surface; transparent plastic sheet with grid divisions. This permits clean guidance for knives without blunting the blade
- universal pair of scissors
- pair of tweezers
- pocket saw with various different saw blades and

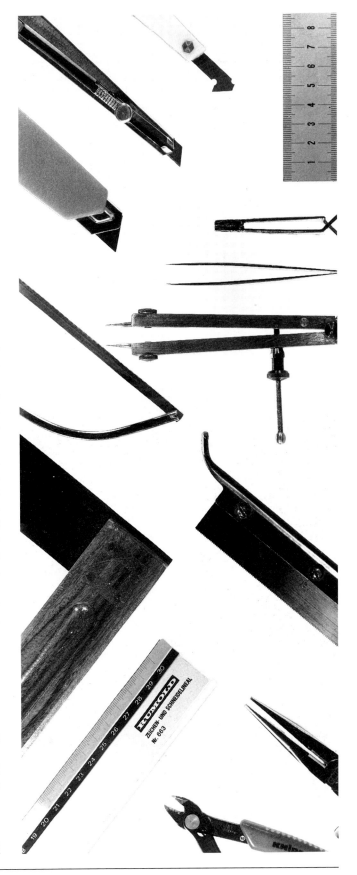

adjustable grip
- tenon-saw with exchangeable blades for use with wood, metal and plastics
- mitre set
- semicircular cross-section flat pair of pliers
- edge cutter
- a set of key files
- small semicircular cross-section wood rasp
- engraving needle
- tracing wheel
- tracing paper
- pencils
- various glues and adhesives
- various adhesive tapes
- double-sided adhesive foils
- folding device
- small rubber roller
- pins
- various sandpapers and emery papers
- grindstone
- spray-grating and toothbrush
- various paintbrushes

This basic set can be augmented by the following machinery and equipment:

- soldering iron and fittings
- thermal-saw (for solid models and site models)
- hand-held drilling machine, preferably with electronic speed control
- power tenon-saw
- sanding machine
- hot-air blower (for bending of methacrylate sheeting and rapid drying of paints)

Eight categories for expansion of tool collection

Measurement, marking out and tracing
- steel rulers, 50 and 100 cm in length
- protractor
- adjustable marking-out gauge
- depth gauge
- metal set-squares with angles of 45° and 60°
- set-squares with adjustable angles
- circular gauges; fixed circle markers and cutters with adjusting screw
- circular proportional gauges
- marking-out needles

Cutting and material separation
- various cutters
- cutting ruler and angle (made in metal with rubber on the underside)
- straight and curved sheet-metal shears. Never cut wire with such shears, because small grooves are worn on

the blades, which then make it impossible for clean edges to be cut
- set of chisels
- set of round chisels
- fretsaw with various saw blades
- handsaw for cutting metal and wood
- small metal saw

Filing, grinding and sanding
- set of files for key-cutting
- flat, semicircular and round files for metal and wood
- flat, semicircular and round rasps (hand-held)

Aids for attachment, holding, adjustment, etc.
- pins
- various pairs of tweezers
- mirrors
- clips
- various clamps
- mitring clamps and clips
- vice grips
- bench vice
- surfaces for assembly of models. Thick plywood coated with plastic. Better still are flat plates made from stone or metal
- angle vices for assembly
- assembly block: cubes or rectangular blocks made from veneered slabs can be home-made and filled with lead or scrap steel pieces. Nails can also be used for this purpose. These blocks are used for attachment, adjustment and loading, when adhesives are allowed to set

Soldering
- electrically-heated soldering iron with various bits. Better still, a complete set of soldering irons
- alternative type: gas-heated soldering equipment
- solder, soldering paste
- flux for soldering
- small brush for application of flux

Painting
- various paintbrushes: flat or round
- spray-grating and brush (old toothbrush)
- porcelain mixing palette
- various containers: glasses, bottles
- spray-gun and compressor
- masking tape and masking foil

Sharpening
- grindstone: rough and fine
- oil-stone for final sharpening of knives and other tools

General tools
- various hammers (light hammer (100 g) – heavy hammer (500 g))

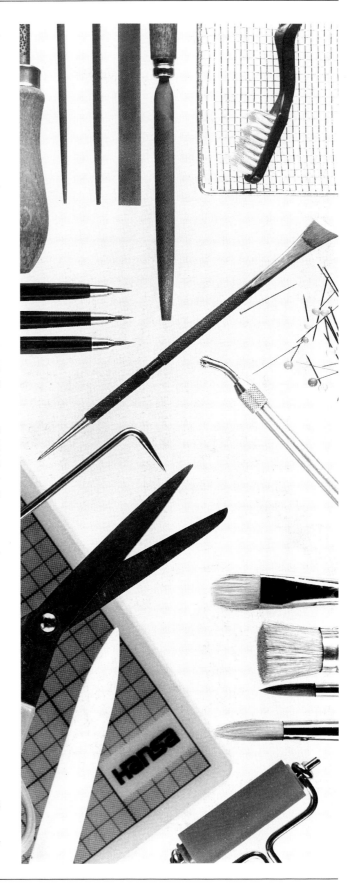

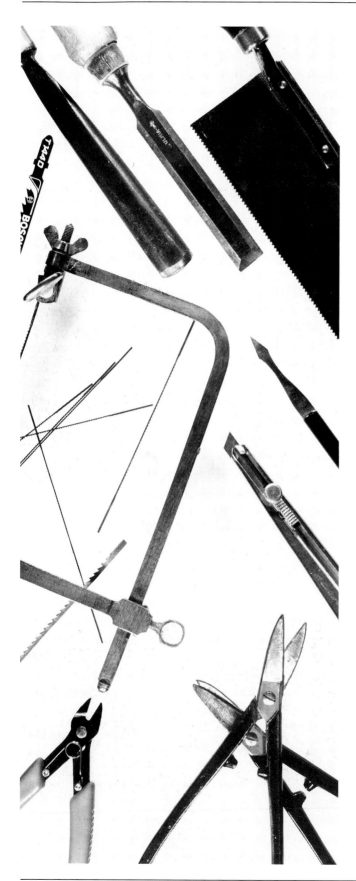

– rubber hammer
– small mallet
– rubber roller for laminating and gluing paper, cardboard, foils, veneers, etc.
– a set of watchmaker's screwdrivers
– spanners
– various flat and round pairs of pliers

3.3 Machinery

It cannot be over-emphasized that fast-running machinery which incorporates sharp tool bits must be operated with great care and undivided attention to prevent injuries. This applies particularly to circular-saws, milling machines, lathes, and the fabrication of small and very small components.

There are combination machines, just as there are combination tools. It is necessary to make a compromise, which sometimes is not too successful in practice. There are, however, some quite useful developments now occurring in this field.

For mounting the machines it is necessary to have a special area, or better still, a special room. It must be well-lit and ventilated. If the machines are being used most days, it is best to fit a stationary dust extraction plant. Otherwise a vacuum cleaner with the appropriate fittings may be sufficient. There must be sufficient bench space next to the machines to make room for working components and drawings. The following machines are adequate for the fabrication of all exhibition-standard models for competitive tendering, exhibitions and demonstration purposes. They also constitute the basis of a small model-building workshop within an architect's office.

Small bench circular-saw
With a width of operation of 40–50 cm.

Care must be taken that the lengthwise guide extends well outside the saw blade so that it is possible to position the work piece correctly along its entire length. In the same way, cross pieces must also permit the work piece to be guided fully and securely. The angle between the saw blade and the work bench, which is normally 90°, should be capable of adjustment. This is achieved by turning the saw blade, or by tilting the surface of the work bench. In the latter case, the bench circular-saw should have an adjustment device in order to reposition the bench surface, together with motor and saw blade, horizontally. With such an arrangement it becomes possible to make slanting cuts for roof inclinations on the bench circular-saw. It is also recommended that the motor is adjusted to operate at different speeds. It this can be done it becomes possible to saw timber, plastics, methacrylate sheeting and non-ferrous metals correctly.

Important components of a bench circular-saw are the various saw blades, with different sizes of teeth, widths and diameters. Do not use quenched high-carbon steel saw blades. The material is brittle and can

break if overloaded or maltreated. Hard metal saw blades with fine teeth are suitable for most materials. Fine and very fine metal saw blades, made from high-carbon steel which has been tempered afterwards by heating until red hot, are suitable for fine cutting and grooving of profiles.

All saw blades used for such purposes should be marked and only used for fine work and not for rough cutting or sawing of plywood and solid timber. Blunt saw blades can be re-sharpened by specialist firms. A bench circular-saw should be connected to a dust extraction device.

Disc grinding machine

Diameter of disc: 30–40 cm, with integrated dust suction or dust bag. The disc grinding machine is fixed

71 Small parts (cars 1:200) are shaped as a lath profile and cut off.

73 Cross-section on the circular-saw. Small parts which have been cut away must be able to come off at the side. If several parts of equal length are needed, the distance between saw blade and a wooden distance piece is adjusted accordingly. Take care that the wooden distance piece is well to the side of the saw blade, and that the small objects produced cannot jam.

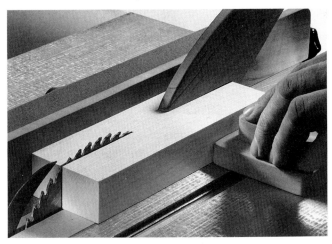

72 Lengthwise section on the circular-saw. The work piece, which lies flat and at a right angle to the guide, is pressed with a piece of wood against the guide and pushed along it with a push rod. Never guide piece from the top or from behind the saw blade!

74 Lengthening of guide. Very small components, which cannot be held safely on the cross guide, are laid against a wooden auxiliary piece. In this way the part has a safe base over its entire length.

onto a tilting surface of a work bench or to an adjustable sliding frame. It is very useful if the motor can be switched to run either clockwise or anticlockwise. The grinding discs are obtainable with different degrees of roughness. They should be changed frequently because only new and sharp grinding discs give smooth surface areas, without needing additional time-consuming work. The grinding discs are attached by means of a special adhesive to the plate-shaped revolving disc of the machine. The adhesive supplied enables the grinding discs to be changed quickly. Other adhesives should not be used.

Bench drilling machine

This incorporates an adjustable table, and permits various depths of drilling and drill speeds. The bench drilling machine is fastened firmly to the bench surface. The drill table must be adjustable and carry a vice. The work piece to be drilled cannot be held by hand in all cases, because there is often a real danger of injury. The chuck must be able to accommodate drill bits at least between 0.5 to 10 mm in diameter.

To drill wood, plastics, methacrylate sheeting and non-ferrous metals correctly, it is not only necessary to use different drill bits, but also to be able to control the speed of the drill. Details regarding the correct speed for the material to be drilled are given in the instruction manual issued by the manufacturer.

Mechanical fretsaw

This is used for cutting wood, plastics and soft metals. It is mainly used to fabricate the various layers for site models. The method of work is similar to that used with a hand fretsaw. There is a smaller version with a reach of 500 mm. A bridge-type version with a combined reach of 1000 mm can be used for larger models. As the cost of the two versions is roughly the same it is best to go for the bridge-type version, provided enough floor space is available.

Thermal-saw

This is used for cutting foamed plastics by means of an electrically heated wire. A suitable piece of equipment should include a rigid arm, with adequate cutting height, accurate lengthwise and crosswise guides, as well as a circle-cutting device. A blower should be available to remove noxious vapours, while switching the wire on and off should be carried out by a foot-operated pedal. This permits the positioning of the work piece with both hands.

Small-scale machines

Small-scale machines are now on the market which have been specially developed for model construction. These machines are most suitable for work involving almost-finished models, and for work on very small parts. The following machines are suitable for our purposes:

- drilling machine with adjustable speed, various drill bits, grinding wheels and sanding wheels
- key-hole saw which can be controlled electronically
- flexible sander
- gas soldering iron

Additional equipment

If it is felt that the workshop should be extended still further, the following machines may be considered:

- guillotine with minimum size DIN A1
- hand band-sanding machine
- band-saw
- surface milling machine
- lathe
- tool-sharpening machine
- adjustable assembly table

Instructions for working with machines

For work involving the bench circular-saw, the disc grinding machine, and the bench drilling machine, it is imperative to read the general work and safety rules. It is also essential to peruse very carefully the specific operating instructions issued by the manufacturers. In addition, the following 14 points should be observed:

1 Tables upon which machines are mounted must always be kept empty and clean. Never put anything down on them. Bench surfaces are often coated with a lubricant to enable work pieces to be moved easily. Saw blades, sanding discs and drill bits must always be kept sharp. When changing saw blade discs you must ensure that the machine cannot be switched on by accident. Disconnect either the plug or the fuse.

2 Take care always to work with first-rate materials. Never use scrap wood, which could contain nails or screws, or even sand and stones. All of these would ruin your tools. Larger pieces of solid timber should be pre-cut by a carpenter to dimensions which can be handled safely by your own bench circular-saw.

3 Very small model components should always be made as parts of larger work pieces. They are cut off from these only when completed.

4 When cutting work pieces from solid wood, make sure that the timber is supported on a clean, flat and perpendicular base. Otherwise there may be a danger of recoil, with poor edges being formed as a result.

5 Work pieces must always be pushed forwards, ahead of the revolving saw blade, and never pulled from behind it. This means that your hands are well clear of the revolving saw blade, which is not the case if you pull the work piece from behind. If you are dealing with small objects, make some wooden push rods so that you can move the small objects safely between the revolving saw blade and the guide.

6 Never use metal objects to push work pieces through. The accident rate from doing so is very high.

7 Never use the lengthwise and crosswise guides at the same time. The section of the work piece which has been separated off must move freely and fall out at the side. Otherwise there is a danger that it may get stuck, causing a jammed saw blade disc, which could damage the motor, break the saw blade, or simply eject the work piece. If both guides have to be used at the same time, i.e. the crosswise guide to lead the work piece along, and the lengthwise, guide to act as a stop, the correct method would be to attach a distance piece to the lengthwise guide, which finishes in front of the saw blade.

8 Small parts are hard to hold firm and can easily get jammed. If small parts are to be cut using the crosswise guide of the saw, it is best to use a long auxiliary lath. The part is fixed to this, which provides a base over its whole length, so that the object which is being made is held securely without any risk of jamming. The saw blade saws through the work piece and also cuts into the auxiliary lath.

9 Adjust the saw blade to the correct height. With normal cuts the saw blade should not protrude more than 6–10 mm from the top of the work piece.

10 When a work piece is sanded using a disc grinder, it should always be held in such a way that the movement of the grinding disc is downwards in relation to the object. If the work piece is held on the other side the grinding dust is thrown up into the air, and the work piece can be ripped out of one's hand. There is also considerable danger of the operator suffering eye injuries.

11 During the grinding or sanding process, the work piece should be moved around in order to prevent grooves being formed, and to avoid carbonizing the surface.

12 If very small components are to be sanded with a disc grinding machine, a wooden supporting piece must always be used. This can be made from solid timber or from chipboard. The wooden support is laid against the sander, and the small part laid on top of it and sanded down. In this way the distance between the disc and the table surface is bridged sufficiently to give the object a secure base.

13 If a bench drilling machine is used to drill through smaller work pieces, or if larger-diameter drill bits are used, the work piece must always be secured by means of a vice or clamps. The work piece should be laid on a base of either chipboard or plywood. This prevents both damage to the bench surface by the drill and splitting of the under-side of the work piece.

14 When small objects are being dealt with, it is always necessary to plan ahead and fabricate the appropriate aid devices for the work which is to be carried out. These may be push rods, supports, or extension guides, etc., and should always be made from wood. These auxiliary components must then be used as close as possible to the cutting tool (saw blade or grinding disc).

75 When using the plate sanding machine, small parts are laid onto a wooden base, so that they are not pulled into the gap between the table and the sanding wheel.

76 Auxiliary pieces for safe working of small components. Distance piece, push rod and wooden pressure piece.

4 The Working Area

Architectural models are an integral part of the study of architecture, and are constructed in both small and large architectural offices. They are not only made as conceptual models and work models for internal use. Exhibition quality models may be used for work connected with obtaining degrees or diplomas, for competitive tenders, and for presentations in which the architect may be involved.

The money and time required to have the model made by a professional model-maker are not always available. Some models have to be finished in a few days for use at conferences. We may also wish to develop our design with the help of the model, and to study and test it. Because of this, it is advisable right at the start to find a suitable place for model-building. The area where the work is to be carried out must not be cramped. Trying to work in a cramped area with sharp tools and machines soon leads to dangerous situations. If storage space is limited, a mess is created which tends

77 Simple work bench for model-building. Tool trolley, cutting board, adjusting board, vice. Places for depositing brushes, scissors, and small pieces of equipment. Power outlets, assembly block, lamps.

to hinder creativity. Thought must also be given to the fact that flammable materials and solvents will be worked with, and that model-building often creates noise, dust and smells which may be objectionable to other people.

In general, the area used for model-building must be well-lit and ventilated. There must be an adequate number of individually-fused power outlets. A main switch and main fuse must be positioned in the work room. There should also be water connections for both cold and hot water, with a substantial sink, close to the working area. In addition, the area needs a comprehensive first aid kit and a fire extinguisher, both of which should be fixed to the wall in a prominent position.

4.1 The initial working area

A work bench situated next to the drawing board is usually adequate for the beginner. It must be big enough to allow the following three operations to take place:

1 An area with cutting base surface, and room for a T-square for the preparation, cutting-out and finishing of the components of the model.
2 An area with a firm, flat surface (see above), for assembly and correct positioning of the various components.
3 An area where tools and small hand-held machines can be put down. To ensure that materials and tools are readily accessible, shelving and a tool chest are required, or better still a tool trolley. Papers, carton, cardboard, plastic sheets (polystyrene and methacrylates), should be protected from dust by storing them horizontally in a chest of drawers. If the worst comes to the worst, use folders for drawing papers. Space is also required for various test-pieces, small

components, and other materials. If there is enough room, a further storage area is highly desirable. This may either be a table, or a board resting on two trestles. A special assembly table with adjustable working height is even better. This enables one to work on the model while standing up straight. Work can become very tiring if one has to sit down, or bend over while standing up. In addition, if the model is on the assembly table it can be viewed from a pedestrian's point of view, allowing important perspective properties to be developed.

By using this type of model-building studio, equipped with the tools and machines recommended for the beginner, the architectural student or designer will be able to deal with most kinds of work. Conceptual and work models, and even many exhibition models, can be made to the standards desired.

4.2 The extended workshop

Once our model-building requirements have expanded, and several larger machines have been acquired, the need for more sophisticated facilities soon arises. Special areas, or even rooms, are then necessary:

1 for the preparation and finishing of part of the model
2 for assembly
3 for material, inspection components, test-pieces, and bits and pieces
4 for machines and tools

Areas for 1 to 3 can all be in the same room. There must be sufficient storage space available, comprising shelves and tables. The machinery room, with electric power outlets, water connections and suitable dust extraction equipment, should be apart from the other room.

5 Preparation of Work

Conceptual models are developed at the same time as sketches and drawings, and require no special preparation, which would hinder rather than help the development of the design in model form. All that is necessary is to have the work bench next to the drawing board with the following items to hand:

– basic tool collection (Section 3.2)
– various basic materials: cardboard, corrugated cardboard, balsa-wood, small wooden profiles
– bits and pieces, remnants from previous models, methacrylate sheeting
– various kinds of adhesives.

Different criteria apply when work models and exhibition models are to be constructed.

5.1 Check-list

Before starting work it is as well to develop a clear idea of what is required. A check-list helps to ensure that nothing is forgotten.

The check-list comprises nine different items:

1 Type of model:
   What kind of model is to be built, and what is it supposed to do? (Chapter 2: Types of Model)
2 Purpose of model:
   What is to be represented?
   What should be investigated and tested?
   Which main aspects of the design or design concept should be conveyed?
   Can these thoughts only be conveyed by a model, or would sketches and drawings be sufficient?
   Should a relationship between the set of plans and model be made?
   Should the building structure be represented on its own, or set within its surroundings and existing buildings?
   Should the model of the building permit inspection of internal features, or should only the external shape be shown?
   Should it be possible to take the building model to pieces, in order to show internal arrangements? If so, should it be possible to take every floor to pieces, or only the roof, single façade wall, etc.?
3 Persons to be addressed:
   To whom is the model to be directed?

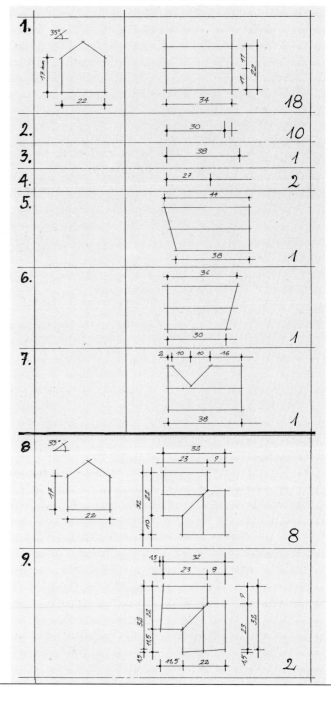

78 Complete and clear list of components with accurate model dimensions for cutting building sections.

To which user should the model serve as an explanation of the intended design?

Will the details of the model be explained by the author (student or architect), or should it be self-explanatory?

4 Stage of work:

Is it a conceptual model, a work model or an exhibition model?

Should parts of the work model be used later on for the exhibition model (base plate, site representation, existing buildings, etc.)?

Should it be possible to modify the model (alternative designs)?

Should it permit corrections to be made to either the landscape or the building structure itself?

5 Scale and sections:

Which scale is to be employed?

Which section is to be chosen?

6 Materials, tools, machinery; capabilities and experience:

Which materials are to be chosen, and do they correspond with the intended design?

What effect is required with the materials employed?

Make a list of materials to be used (wood, cardboard, methacrylate sheeting, etc.)

Surfaces of materials (smooth, rough, reflecting, etc.)

Colours (coloured or plain). Is it possible to get hold of sufficient quantities of the materials needed in the time available? Is it possible to work with the desired materials using the tools and machines available and the work area at our disposal?

Are the right tools, machines, knowledge and experience available in order to carry out such work? If in doubt, make some test samples.

7 Packaging and transport:

How is the model to be packed up and transported? Is it necessary to be able to take the model apart?

8 Working data:

Is all requisite information available? (topographic plans, floor areas, sections and views)

Are the plans in the correct scale for use in the model? Are the drawings for model-building suitable for immediate construction of the model? Are the main characteristics of the design suitable for the materials, tools, machinery, ability and experience available? Do the drawings represent the essential contours for model-building? Are there sufficient copies of the set of plans available for building the model? Extra ones will be needed for the production of smaller parts.

The scale of a model depends largely upon the restrictions of size. The table (right) gives the size of houses and squares when different scales are chosen.

Have lists of components (for example, when building town models) been drawn up? What kind of wooden profiles are needed, and how are they to be cut so that it is always possible to handle the work piece securely? What is the best order of work when making special components, and which auxiliary devices (push rods, fitting pieces, etc.) do we require?

For example: first cut with circular-saw, drilling, second cut with circular-saw, sanding, cleaning of surface and painting, assembly and building into the site model.

9 Final check:

Before starting work, check tools, machinery, the materials necessary, and look through the set of plans. If the tools available or other conditions make it impossible to fabricate the model or parts of it oneself, the work may have to be given to a specialist model-making firm. It is then necessary to explain to them in exact detail what the model is supposed to represent, and to listen to and discuss their counter-proposals, until a firm decision is made.

It pays to prepare the working data in a form suitable for model-building right from the start. This should only contain the information needed for the model, not the projected building. To work through a whole set of building plans and then to build the model of it to a scale of, say, 1:500 wastes a lot of time, and can also lead to misunderstandings and wrong interpretations. However, the information given must not be too scrappy. The model-builder needs to have a comprehensive understanding of the completed design.

Scales

The scale used depends upon the total size of the model, i.e. the maximum area available for it. The table shown below gives some indication of how given buildings and ground areas should be represented when various scales are used.

Example	1:50	1:100	1:200	1:500
Kiosk 4×2×3 m	80×40×60	40×20×30	20×10×15	8×4×6 mm
Single-family home 16×12×18 m	320×240×160	160×120×80	80×60×40	32×24×16 mm
Multiple-family home 32×12×18 m	700×240×360	350×120×180	175×60×90	70×24×36 mm
Office block 50×15×80 m	1000×300×1600	500×150×800	250×75×400	100×30×160 mm
Small square 60×80 m	1200×1600	600×800	300×400	120×160 mm
Large square 160×200 m	3200×4000	1600×2000	800×1000	320×400 mm

6 Fabrication of Components

Architectural models are made one step at a time. These stages can be summarized as follows:

- construction of the base plate
- development of the topography, i.e. the shape of the site
- positioning of green, traffic and water surfaces
- fabrication of building structure
- insertion of the building structure into its surroundings
- insertion of plants and scale impression-giving parts
- labelling
- protective cover: packaging

It is up to the model-builder whether he or she keeps strictly to this order of construction, or whether to start with the building and then make the base plate and the surroundings. It is only important that the model is considered in its entirety, and that the message it is intended to convey, in the form of an overall concept, is not lost.

6.1 The base plate

Five different aspects must be observed when making and shaping the base plate:

- the model section must be made rigid
- it should emphasize the model against its surroundings, and present the shape of the model as an independent expression and reality
- it is necessary to plan how the model is to be labelled
- it should be possible to transport the model if necessary. If the model is to be shifted, it should be possible to take the model apart, and a protective cover should be devised
- construction materials and methods of making the various layers representing the contours and substrata should be considered, along with materials for making the building structure itself, and how these parts are attached to the base plate. Included in this are representations of areas below ground level, such as

foundations, underground garages, underground passages, etc.

6.1.1 Model section

The shape and size of the base plate does not only depend upon the scale of the model and the resulting dimensions. It is also determined by whether we want the design to stand on its own, or whether it is to be integrated into an existing ensemble. In this respect, both the intended shape and the desired impression to be made affect the positioning on the base plate.

Both contour layers and the building structures themselves can border directly onto the base plate. They can also be positioned away from the edge, or they can stand freely upon it. The shape of the base plate can be either:

- square or rectangular
- in the form of a polygon (regular or irregular)
- in the shape of the site area upon which the building stands
- a curved shape (circular or with free curves)

A rectangle is the most common shape used for making a base plate, because it is easy to fabricate, transport and pack.

The rectangle should not be considered simply as a rigid shape, but also as a kind of interplay between forces, a type of movement. Each one expands, and has a preferred direction. This force counteracts the restrictions of the boundaries. The forces of expansion and boundary restriction produce a situation which can be read as a directional movement, i.e. either as a horizontal or vertical rectangle. The direction of movement is described by the ratio of the sides. A square base plate does not possess this directional tendency. Its focal point lies at its centre. With regular polygons and circles the action is concentrated at one single point, the geometric centre.

If a single building, or a group of houses, is positioned on a base plate, it becomes a part of this interplay of forces. The shape and size of the base plate can strengthen directions of the design, either by neutralizing or accentuating them. The centre of a projected design, for example a town square or a central room, can become the focal point. By its position on the base plate, which has been shaped accordingly, this can be accentuated and made more obvious. Zones close to the edge can be contrasted with central ones.

The shape of the base plate also affects the direction from which the model should be viewed. If squares or circles are used as concentric shapes this provides no preferred viewing direction, and the design can easily be turned on its axis and viewed from all sides. With rectangular or free shapes a distinct viewing direction is emphasized, and constitutes a clear invitation to view the model from one given direction and no other.

6.1.2 Subframe and base

For presentation purposes the whole model should become one entity and stand out against its surroundings. It should be supported on its own frame or on a specially-made base unit. Combinations of design are also possible.

Feet

It should be possible to elevate the base plate in its display position, even if it is only resting on small rubber pads, like the ones used for stereo equipment in the electronics industry. The other extreme would be to provide a table frame, with the base plate as the table top. The frame and legs can be separated visually from the base plate by a shadow gap. The height of the legs is determined by the use to be made of the model and the position where it is to be exhibited. It can be placed at chair height, table height, level with the eyes, or above eye level. In fact, it can be placed in any position, from a bird's-eye view to a view slightly below eye level, depending on what is needed.

79   The model section in this case is governed by the shape of the site. Scale: 1:100. Base plate: 13 mm chipboard. Height contour layers: 2 mm Finnish cardboard, built in full layers. Building: 1mm–2mm Finnish cardboard. Loadbearing structure: closed cube; perforated relief section façade with grey coloured paper at back. Window transoms and mullions drawn in, with window shutters attached. Green features: small bare twigs.

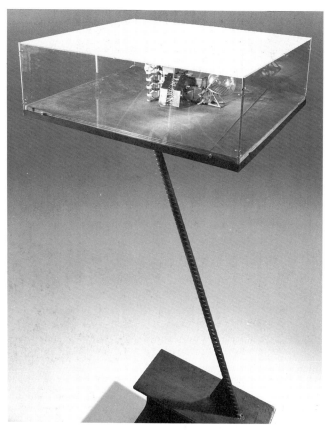

80 Model scale, 1:200. Example of an unusual presentation of a model. Foot: girder with welded steel beam. Base plate: 20 mm layered plate. Buildings made from wire, metal sheeting, glass. Protective cover from methacrylate sheeting.

81 Presentation of a floor relief at height of observer (about 110 cm): placed on a closed base on top of a frame support.

Base unit

A base, connected to the outside of the base plate, is made from roof battens, boards with straight upper edges, or rectangular section steel tubing. It stabilizes the base plate against deformation and warping, and elevates the model from the table or floor. If areas in excess of DIN A1 are involved, a wooden grid framework is screwed or glued to the underside of the base plate. If the model is to be capable of being taken to pieces, the base plate must be stiffened in this way. If a second plate is fixed to this frame, one side can be left open, and the space in between can be used to keep explanatory drawings. Alternatively, it is possible to place objects there which lie underneath the level of the terrain. With larger base plates distance pieces should be fixed between the two areas of the frame. As where legs are used, the base can be any desired height: anything from 2 cm up to table or eye level.

Frame

A model acts like a relief map, or in some cases rather more like a picture. Just as with a relief map or a picture, the model is put in a frame. The frame should be formed in such a way that it not only emphasizes the model and forms its border, but also protects the base plate against damage. It should stand out clearly against the model to provide an optical contrast.

Covering the sides of the surfaces is necessary because the edges of most materials used for the construction of the base plate always need some sort of treatment. Methacrylate sheeting, when used as a base plate, must be ground and polished on all sides. Chipboard or plywood sheets have to be covered at the edges, or edge strips must be attached. It is also possible to paint or spray the edges with emulsion paint, acrylics, lacquers etc.

Edge strips

Edge strips are usually made from the same material as the top surface of the base plate or the layers representing the terrain. If another material is chosen, the edge strip acts like a frame. If the layers forming the terrain are made from wood, the edge strips should be made from the same type of wood and formed in such a way that the whole gives the effect of having been made from a single block of timber. After assembly it is necessary to sand everything, either using a machine or by hand.

If the height contour layers are not full ones, the edge of the model does not form a closed area and the edge strips are glued on after assembly of the contour layers. Before this is done, the edges of the base plate and the height layers should be sanded. The edge strip is then fitted against the height layers, glued on and sanded.

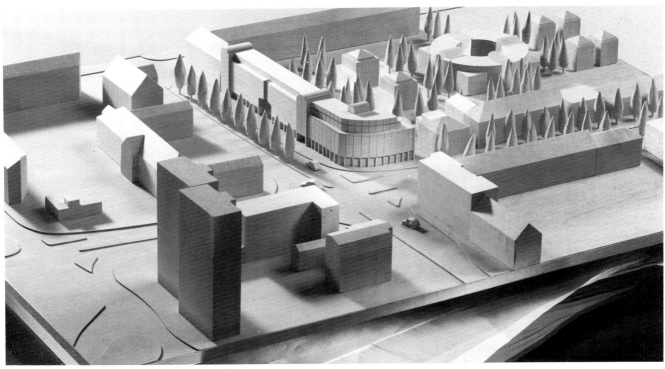

Edging

Fixing of edges is always necessary when the edge strip does not fit properly against the surface of the base plate, or is made from a different material. It is not essential that the edging follows the different height levels of the terrain layers. Fixing the edging is always the first step of the framing process.

6.1.3 Lettering

It is important to letter exhibition models and, particularly, presentation models. Lettering encompasses everything from a general description of the object, down to single pieces of information, such as street names and height of the terrain.

The following labels are essential:

- name of project
- scale and compass direction indicator
- name of originator or code number of competitor (competitive tendering)

This information can be:

- on a special place reserved for lettering
- on part of the frame or outside the frame
- on the protective cover
- freely distributed

Additional information which should be given:

- names of streets and buildings

82 Town planning model, 1:500. Base plate: 8 mm plywood with double floor to permit storage of plans. Site: relief traffic area made from 1 mm aircraft plywood. Buildings from lime timber. Trees made from lime timber, shaped as poplars. The new buildings are distinguished from the old ones by the way façades are shown.

- description of use made of specific areas
- description of planted areas
- designation of road and path access, and also of boundaries
- data regarding dimension of height contour layers

It is best if thought is given at as early a stage as possible as to where, how, which size and in which type of script the lettering should be displayed. An area in a corner of the base plate can be reserved for lettering, just as is done with plans. This, however, generally disturbs the visual effect. Equally unsatisfactory is over-sized lettering, or lettering where the colours clash. An example of this would be black letters on a white sticky label, mounted on a dark model. If you do not wish to use hand lettering, use stencils, a typewriter, or single letters made from cardboard or plastic, which are obtainable from major stationery stores.

Text produced by typewriter, a computer, or set in other ways, can be enlarged or reduced by means of a photocopier, or copied onto coloured paper, transparent sheeting or self-adhesive sheeting. Depending upon the character of the model, handwriting or a typewriter should be used for lettering. Work models and models with a spontaneous collage-type effect, are often lettered by hand.

Before putting the first line of lettering permanently onto the model carry out trials to find out the optimum effect. Test the size of the script and its colour, as well as the way it is to be arranged in specific cases. Start with blocks of lettering which should be prominent and are difficult to place. Smaller lettering can then be accommodated quite easily.

6.1.4 Taking model apart, protective cover

Larger models must be capable of being taken apart for transportation. It is important to think carefully about the separation line, bearing in mind that the cut must not go through the building structure. The various components of the base plate need to have a stiff supporting structure, so that they fit together as closely as possible (Section 6.1.2). The sections are joined together with wooden dowels, or the two frames are bolted together with coach bolts and wing nuts.

An effective cover can be made from methacrylate sheeting. Such a cover sits on the frame of the base plate, and can be screwed onto the base plate. If the model is to be transported some distance, the methacrylate cover should be replaced by a cover made from plywood, which also is screwed to the base plate.

6.1.5 Materials used for base plate

The following materials are suitable for the construction of the base plate:

- self-supporting materials, such as thick plywood or thick sandwich board
- materials which need a supporting structure underneath, such as methacrylate sheeting, mirror foil or thin aluminum sheeting
- for smaller areas, carton or lined foamed plastic can be used
- for the first conceptual or work model, the lid of a wooden chest may be adequate
- glass, stone slabs, or any other material which can interpret the designer's concepts

When choosing the material, thought must be given to which structures are going to be fixed to the base plate, and the method of attachment. The base plate should be flat and very rigid in itself. Warping of the base plate is prevented by constructing a supporting structure.

Aluminium sheeting, mirror foils, methacrylate sheeting and similar flexible materials require a rigid support structure. This may be a thick slab of chipboard, or

very thick multiple-layered plywood. It is possible to drill into this from the top and screw objects to it at the bottom. If the base plate is allowed to protrude a few centimetres at the periphery the supporting framework is hidden. The model of the building then appears to stand on the thin material. Any protruding edges of glass sheeting must be ground down to prevent injuries.

6.2 The site area

The site area is built up on the base plate, the shape and dimensions of which should be decided at the same time as the nature of the model section. Several questions have to be answered before the site area is constructed. The answers are of importance not only when choosing between materials, the type of tools used and the techniques used for building the models. They also dictate the effect of the completed model.

6.2.1 Final form or modifiable?

The material must be light and easily-worked if the model is at the design stage, and is to be used for the study of any of the following:

- modulation of the terrain
- how approaches should be formed
- formation of embankments
- supporting walls
- staircases and ramps
- ground connections of buildings

For conceptual and work models, the following materials are suitable because they can be easily modified:

- clay
- 'Plasticine'
- corrugated cardboard
- cardboard
- foamed plastics, etc.

If, however, the shape of the site area, the position of the building structure, and the roads and paths are already fixed in the appropriate plans, the base plate and site are made in a similar way to an exhibition model. Some exhibition models may need to be constructed to allow minor corrections to be made. This has to be considered when the substructure is designed. It must be possible to re-cut the height line or to shift a building without ruining the whole model.

If methacrylate sheeting or aluminium sheeting have been chosen, every change and correction will mean a new site model as these materials cannot be worked after they have been cut and assembled.

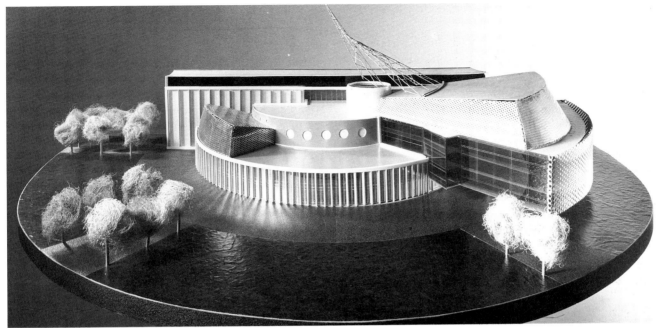

6.2.2 Natural or abstract?

Either a natural or an abstract formulation of the existing buildings and the new structures can be sought, depending upon the way we wish to portray the building; traffic, green and water surfaces; built-up areas; planted areas and scale, impression-forming items. The natural or abstract effect is not achieved merely by use of either 'artificial' or 'natural' materials. It may be the choice of either wooden balls or bits of dried-up sheep's wool to express trees. In general, this is decided by the fundamental nature of the model to be made.

A terrain constructed using fabrics and gypsum will appear more natural than one which is made as a stepwise laminate structure. There are all kinds of intermediate stages between a completely natural model, of the type used in railway model-building, down to the completely abstract treatment, where an inclined piece of aluminium sheeting represents a green area, and a forest is shown as a collection of steel pins.

6.2.3 Blending or contrasting?

The following question must always be answered: how is the relationship between the existing structures and the new buildings to be represented in the model? The answer to this determines whether the new buildings and the new open area can blend in visually. Alternatively, the new building structures can be represented in a contrasting style by using different materials, working methods, details and colours. 'Blending or contrasting' refers in this case to the difference between old and

83 Scale: 1:200. Base plate: 22 mm chipboard. Site made from structured 'Resopal'. Buildings: roofs from 1 mm polystyrene; façades from coloured methacrylate, polystyrene, various types of perforated metal sheeting, PVC supports, soldered construction. Trees: steel wool on 4 mm wooden dowels. The semicircular base plate accentuates the radial arrangement of the building.

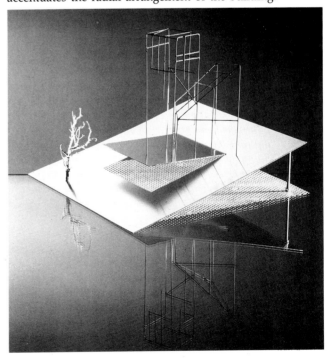

84 Strongly abstract representation of a site. Base plate: perforated aluminium sheeting with threaded rods. Site: 1 mm aluminium sheeting hinged on to design plane. Space structure: soldered wire. Dried thyme twig as tree.

new in the model, and not to differences in the design itself, such as building lines, heights, etc.

It is not uncommon to over-do, or even fake, the way the new building fits into the existing picture. A tall block, when represented by floors only, against the existing structures which are shown in generalized masses, may then appear to be environmentally acceptable when this is not the case.

Blending-in and contrast are achieved by the choice of materials, surface treatment, methods of building the model, and degree of detail.

If these are the same, the new structures will appear to blend in with those that already exist. It is also possible to reduce the contrast between different materials, such as aluminium and polystyrene, by adopting a similar degree of detailing.

6.2.4 Scale and materials

The choice of materials is also affected by the scale used. Wood with strong graining can dominate because of its colour and surface texture to such an extent that neither the shape and size of the building nor the site relief can be properly judged or assessed. Rough and strongly-structured materials are particularly unsuited to city models with a scale of 1:500 or less. As the plastic shape of the site relief becomes most obvious when pale to white colours are used, it is best to choose light colours for the model. If necessary, the site model can be sprayed with white paint or stippled with a stippling brush. On the other hand, a dark-coloured site model, made from pear wood, dark stained wood, bituminous

soft fibre slabs or similar, can set off the white model of a building in a quite magnificent way. In every case the person concerned with the building of the model should test, right at the beginning, how colours and materials will blend. He or she should also test which combination comes closest to the required result.

If the contoured site is made in the form of layers, the thickness of material used for this must be appropriate to the scale used in the model. If, for example, the heights are given in steps of 1 metre, this means, in the case of a layered model with a scale of 1:100, a material thickness of 10 mm. In order to reduce the step-like and very coarse overall impression, it is possible to insert intermediate layers, which are interpolated according to the plans. A suitable method, in the case of our example, is to change each 1 metre step into five steps, each 20 cm thick. In our model, this means a material thickness of 2 mm. Depending upon the overall concept, the model-builder should have the following materials available for constructing the site model:

- corrugated cardboard
- paper-coated foamed plastic sheeting
- coated cardboard

85 Models, 1:500. Base plates: 8 mm chipboard.
Comparison of design representation in uniform and contrasting styles.
Left: sites from lime timber, buildings using lime and pear timber. Round wooden beading cut at a slant.
Right: Site from 2 mm Finnish cardboard. Buildings from lime timber, partly stippled white, and partly sprayed white/grey. Trees made from paper balls.

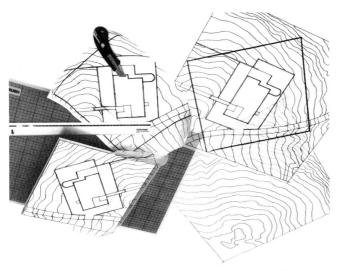

86 Fabrication of topographic models in separate layers. The height contour lines are copied upside down on self-adhesive foil, with the building contours drawn in. The size of the base plate is fixed. The foil is attached to the material forming the height contour layers.

87 The height contour lines are cut out with a fretsaw.

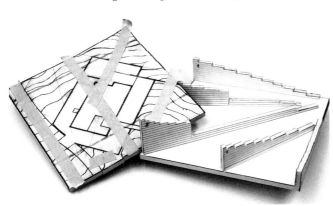

88 Base plate with substructure in the form of terraces.

89 Traffic areas and site areas are shown in squared foil.

90 The assembly of the topographic model. Assembly of the height contour layers and the site area.

91 The finished site with frame and assembled layers.

92 Topographic model in separate layers (3 mm sandwiched EPS). Shown in the uncut state with masking paper in position. Paths treated using a spray-gun.

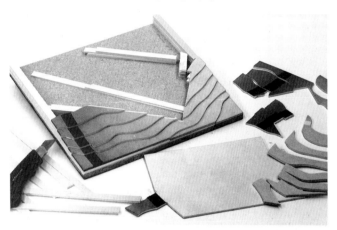

93 Height contour layers cut away by a modelling knife and separated off. Glued onto 8 mm chipboard, with 3 mm sandwiched EPS strips beneath.

94 The complete site model. Separated height contour layers made from sandwiched EPS. Trees made from filter foamed plastic on trunks made from twisted wire.

- bituminized soft fibre panels
- cork slabs
- foamed polyurethanes
- expanded polystyrene
- plywood
- solid polystyrene
- methacrylate sheeting
- metal sheeting (aluminium, brass, etc.)

To get rapid and clean gluing of the various height contour layers, contact adhesives suited to the construction materials concerned are usually employed. However, care should be taken with the solvents in these adhesives; test the glues first, wear a breathing mask, and make sure there is adequate ventilation.

The next stage entails fabrication of the terrain, for which accurate topographic plans are necessary. These must include the ground on which the buildings will stand, the traffic, green, and water surfaces, as well as the following: large trees, external staircases, ramps, external walls, etc. If new roads are to be built, take care that the height contours always cross the road at a right angle, i.e. there must be no cross gradient. Equally, the height contours form horizontal areas, so that a sectional cut and banking is produced, with the edge of the banking being fixed. When everything is ready, all height contour lines and marked points are then traced onto the material which will form the layers. This is normally carried out using a tracing wheel and tracing needle. With some materials, like cork, copying paper and a tracing pen are used.

A simple way of transferring the drawing with its height contour lines, areas, ramps and so on, to the material used for making the layers is to use copying paper laid onto the plan with the inked side upwards, producing a tracing on the material to be used.

A better method is to make a photocopy of the plan on transparent plastic sheets (the type used for making visual aids), which is then glued onto the surface of the material. This can also be used later on as a template when the model is to be painted. The laminate layers can now be cut from the back of the material. The various building, traffic, green, and water surfaces can be dealt with, either before or after the cutting-out process, but always before assembly.

Depending upon the material used, the terrain layers are cut out with fretsaw, keyhole-saw, tenon-saw, band-saw or thermal-saw. Take care that the working surface (cutting underlay or machine table) is clean and free from grease.

6.2.5 Water surfaces, green areas and traffic areas

First of all, it is necessary to mark roads and footpaths, the contours of parking areas, playgrounds and public areas, as well as the various watercourses, on the surface of the terrain. Various methods are available for treating the surfaces.

Note: The overall impression given by an architectural model is dependent on the accuracy with which traffic and green areas are shown.

Linear representation
The boundary lines are drawn using a sharp, hard pencil (F to 2H). With this it is possible to draw in ground markings, such as traffic direction and bus stops. The area itself is untreated. Alternatively, a steel gouge needle may be used to mark the contours or to engrave them into a homogeous surface. For conceptual and work models it is sufficient to mark the most important lines with pins and threads.

When methacrylate sheets or aluminium sheeting are used, the surface may be engraved and the lines accentuated by rubbing paint into them. The paint is applied by means of a piece of cotton wool or thread-free gauze, and the surface is then rubbed clean once more. The various single contour layers are only cut out after this work has been done. The cut edges are cleaned up and the parts are glued together, one on top of the other.

Surface treatment of different types of areas
The various areas can be made distinguishable from each other by different surface treatment and colour.

A 'collage' treatment may be used. The area concerned, such as a road, is traced onto a piece of coloured paper, cut out, and glued on the material forming the terrain. By skilful selection of the right materials (coloured paper, newspaper, reflective foil, etc.) the various areas in the model can be represented correctly. It is, however, necessary to plan the work ahead from the start. The opposite to 'collage' is 'decollage'. Several layers of papers are glued onto the terrain layer and allowed to dry. Using a knife and a tracing needle, some of the paper is then taken off again. This produces interesting area effects, and may be used to shape some larger surfaces, such a green areas, in a contrasting fashion.

The simplest method of all is to cut the road network from the drawing and pin it to the terrain. It is also possible to cut out various self-adhesive pieces of

95 Relief representation of traffic and green areas. Building consists of rigid foamed plastic, painted white, with façades as glued-on copies of drawings. Trees are made from bottle-brushes.

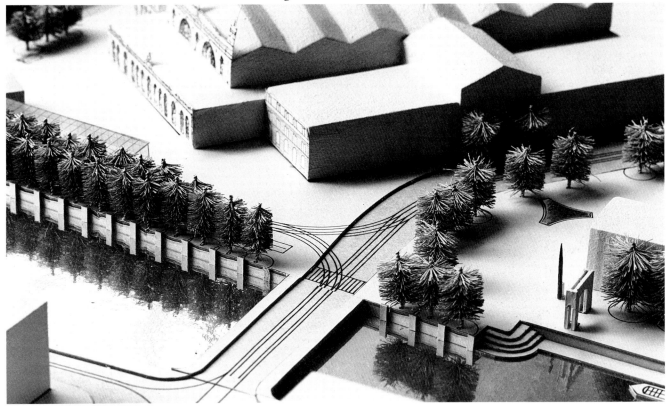

sheeting, and to think out further combinations of materials and colours. But one should not go overboard on all this. Enough is enough.

Painting

Paints can be applied either by brush or spray-gun. A simpler way is to use a brush and a spray-grating. If either a spray-gun or spray-grating are used, it is first of all necessary to mask sections of the model which are not to be coated. Special masking paper with a weak adhesive layer can be bought in suitable shops. This is glued onto the entire layer of the material where sections are to be coated. The areas to be sprayed are then cut out with a sharp knife. It is best to use a special stencil-cutting blade. The masking paper covering the surface to be sprayed is then removed and the exposed area is covered with paint. Care must be taken that the knife blade is sharp and leaves clean edges. Some sensitivity is necessary when cutting the masking paper, so as not to scratch or cut into the material which makes up the layers. Before a new colour is sprayed on, the areas which have already been finished are covered over by newspapers.

Instead of using masking paper, tissue paper tracings of the drawing may also be used, and stencils cut from them. The stencils are then attached with pins as close as possible to the surfaces of the layers. When using a spray-gun a breathing mask must be worn. Instead of spraying paint, we can also use a stippling brush together with tempera or acrylic paint to apply a thin coat. For conceptual or work models it is good enough to paint a path or a road by hand with a flat brush. The network of paths or roads can also be cut out from coloured papers, which are simply laid on top of the layered material and glued on.

Painted surfaces are easily damaged. The various layers should be cut out before the paint has been applied. They can then be assembled and positioned using 'Sellotape'. Paint can then be applied.

Representation as a relief

A more discreet effect is achieved by the treatment of various areas using different textures. Fine surface markings, such as dots, hatching, cross-hatching, etc., can be carried out with a knife or gouge. As the effect depends upon the casting of slight shadows, it is essential to use as light a background as possible.

An alternative method is to cut out the green area or built-up areas from very thin material (paper, thin carton or aircraft plywood), and glue them on before painting them in the same colour as the rest of the surface areas. The roads will then appear depressed below the general level. Again it is the fine shadow along the cut edges which does the trick. To get as uniform an appearance as possible, the height contour layers should only be cut out after they have been treated and glued together.

Water surfaces

Water surfaces can be represented by any of the methods

96 Representation of a water surface: 2 mm cork sheeting, sprayed with silver-bronze. Site made from Plaster of Paris. Trees and bushes made from twisted wire with bits of loofah and Iceland moss.

97 Representation of a water surface. 'Polyfilla' applied with coarse spatula. Site, trees and bushes as with illustration 96.

98 Island, set onto a mirror surface.

99 Island set on top of a sheet of glass, which in its turn rests upon patterned coloured paper.

mentioned above. In many cases, however, one of the following techniques may be more effective:

- sandpaper which has been painted in a silver-bronze colour
- corrugated cardboard, either painted or left in its natural state
- mirror foil
- profiled methacrylate sheeting
- methacrylate sheeting with coloured paper attached underneath
- methacrylate sheeting with an air space between it and the coloured paper underneath it

Coloured paper for such purposes can be made by the model-builder by using a spray-gun to apply a range of light to dark colours to represent the different depths of water.

100 The height contour layers continue underneath the water surface (glass sheet). The depth impression is strengthened by deepening the colour shading.

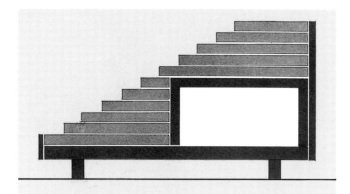

101   Outline of a site construction with complete height contour layers, with a substructure to save material.

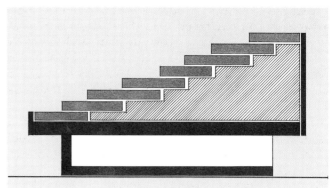

102   Outline of a site construction with overlapping height contour layers. The shaded areas represents the substructure. The base plate has an open cavity for storage of plans.

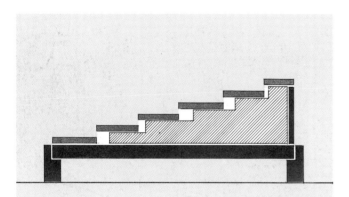

103   Outline of a site construction made from separated layers, set given distances apart. The shaded area indicates the substructure. The base plate is strengthened by a frame.

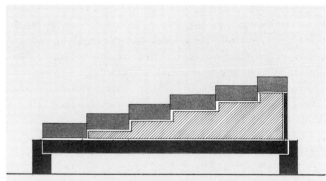

104   Outline of a site construction, using separate height contour layers. The material thickness exceeds the step heights, which are determined by the substructure.

6.2.6 Building up the site using contoured layers

There are three ways in which the site can be built up:

- building up the layers with full, overlapping or separated steps of layers
- inclined surfaces, which can be continuous or made up of separate parts
- free modelling

Building up with layers
Every height contour of the plan represents a layer in the model. The thickness of the material used must correspond in scale with the difference in actual height contours. Interpolation can be carried out (Section 6.2.4).

Full layers
The fabrication of each height contour by a whole sheet requires a lot of material, but is easy to carry out and produces a rigid structure. These are cut, one after the other, from the bottom upwards. They are then glued together using contact adhesive, as indicated in the plan. In order to save weight and material, larger full-layer models include hollow spaces. Part of the internal volume is made from foamed plastics or similar materials. This is a very good solution, particularly for very steep terrain. Full-layer models make further work easy and allow depressions to be cut out subsequently. Depending upon the material used, they can be drilled and sanded. Because of their rigidity they are suitable for use as base plates that can be taken apart.

Overlapping layers
To produce a site model made in this way, only two sheets of the same thickness of material are required. The thickness corresponds to the steps of the height

contours. All height contour lines are traced on to these two sheets and numbered. One of the sheets is then cut along all the even height contour lines, and the other along all the odd ones. The contour which lies more or less in the middle of each strip then serves to locate these strips while they are glued together. Always alternate between sheet A and sheet B.

Such a method of construction saves weight and material. In order to achieve rigidity it requires a sub-structure, which may be somewhat laborious to make. The material must be stiff enough to prevent the individual strips from sagging. Alterations can only be made afterwards provided the material removed is within the range of the overlap.

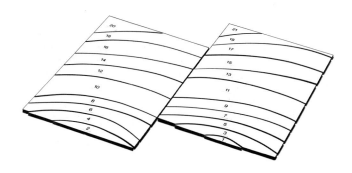

Separate layers

All layers are cut out from a single sheet and are then assembled on a step-wise support structure. The cut edges always form the rear edge of the lower layer and the front edge of the upper layer. If an open impression of the site, where the layers do not touch at the cut edges, is acceptable, the thickness of material used does not really matter. A closed impression can also be achieved with a corresponding thickness of material. The advantages of this method of construction lie not only in the saving of material and weight, but also in speed of fabrication. For this method of construction it is also necessary to use a material which possesses enough stiffness to be self-load bearing, and which does not sag. Cork, soft cardboard and similar materials are unsuitable. A disadvantage of this method is that subsequent modifications become virtually impossible to carry out.

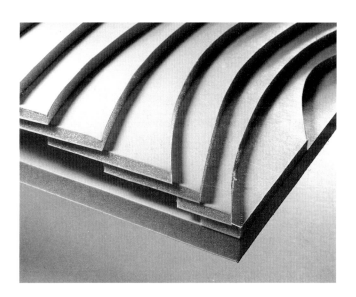

105 Outline for building site models using overlapping layers. Two equally large sheets with the dimensions of the base plate. On the right-hand sheet the odd contour heights are drawn in, while the left-hand plate has the even ones. (*top*)

106 Outline for building site models using overlapping height contour layers. The rear edge of the lower height contour layer corresponds with the upper edge of the next height contour layer above it. (*middle*)

107 Fabrication of a site model using full layers. Material: 2 mm cork. Plan, building material for model, tracing paper and base plate are all cut to the same dimensions. Using the tracing wheel, the height contour lines are transferred from the plan onto the cork, and cut out. (*bottom*)

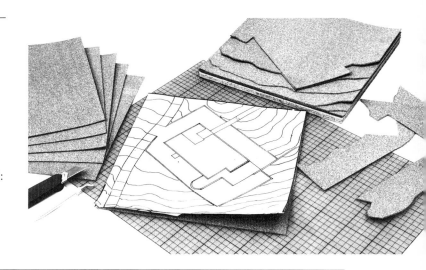

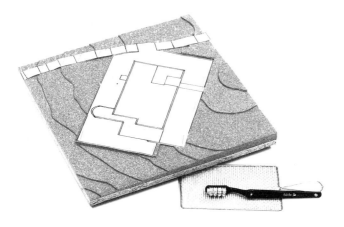

108 The transfer of traffic and green areas. The traffic area, which has been cut out, is pinned firmly on to the topographic model. Using a spray-grating and brush, the colouring matter (stain or emulsion paint) is applied as required for the area in question.

109 The finished site model.

110 Site model made from overlapping height contour layers. The ground plan of the base plate is determined by the site. The height contour layers are levelled by means of threaded rods. Baseplate: 16 mm sandwich timber slab; height contour layers: grey cardboard; trees: nails; buildings: painted solid timber. (*below*)

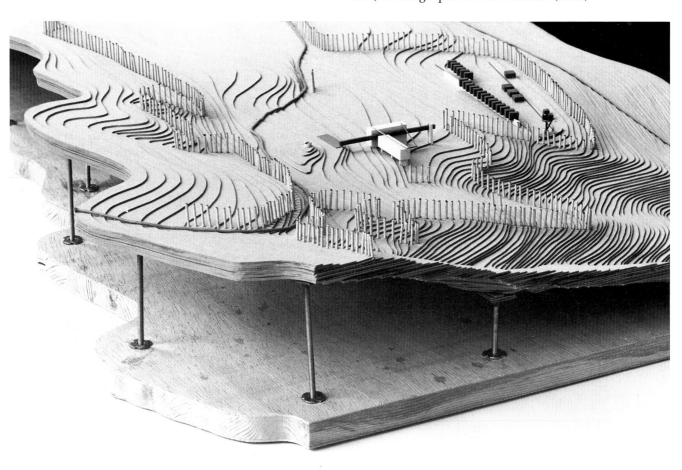

111 Free representation of a site model made from inclined planes, which are set prismatically against each other. Material: 3 mm sandwiched EPS, block of granite.

112 Freely-developed site model. Base plate: chipboard; height contour layers: expanded polystyrene, cut with a thermal-saw along appropriate lines and assembled. The site is then treated with 'Polyfilla' applied with a spatula.

6.2.7 Building with inclined planes

In some cases it is undesirable to represent the terrain of the site model as a stepwise structure. If the site does not possess a strongly modulated relief, inclined areas are a good alternative. If the slope is even there are few problems in representing it as a scaled surface in the model. The only difficulty that may arise is on the side, when the model section runs at a slant to the height contours. To overcome this, measure the heights from the lowest point upwards on the surrounding frame or substructure to which the terrain area is fixed. The connection between the site model and building model must also be made strictly according to the plans.

Sometimes there are two or more terrain areas which have a different slope. This method of construction may be used to depict a strongly abstract, crystalline shape of the site. This may often improve the appearance of the design. Some practice is needed to subdivide the various single areas, to draw their true dimensions and to fit them neatly against each other. Here, too, it is essential to ensure that streets and paths are integrated into the terrain without any cross-slope.

6.2.8 Free modelling of site

Free modelling of the site produces a fairly true and natural representation. Such sites are widely used in model railway design, as well as in the panoramas found in museums and exhibitions. However, such techniques are not often used in architecture.

The freely-modelled site is made in three stages. Firstly a supporting structure is built to show the over-all shape of the site. Materials which are easy to work, such as expanded polystyrene, soft fibre board, foamed plastic boarding or multi-layer corrugated cardboard, are used for such purposes. Next, a woven fabric is stretched over this supporting structure. Typical materials employed may be jute, sacking, gauzes or, alternatively, wire mesh or fly screen gauze. The weaves of sacking or jute are treated with an aqueous glue mix, such as woodworker's glue or wallpaper paste, and tamped down. Everything is then allowed to dry. The next stage is to apply a filler of the type used for car bodywork repairs, with a spatula. In this way the final shape is achieved. Such a model is elastic and relatively lightweight.

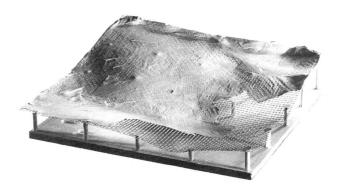

113 Freely-developed site model. The coordinate system is copied onto 10 mm chipboard. Height positions are fixed according to the plan with wooden dowels. Wire gauze is then attached to these, and the whole is coated with papier mâché.

114   Tools and materials for repair and additional work on gypsum (Plaster of Paris) castings: various straight and curved chisels, modelling knife, spatula, water, 'Polyfilla', brush.

115   Wetting of the parts of the gypsum model which have to be taken off. A paint brush is used for this purpose.

116   Removal of slivers of the wetted areas with straight and round-edged chisels. The gypsum casting must be firm. Hold and guide tools with both hands!

If expanded polystyrene is used as a base, there is no need for the fabric layer. Using a knife or a hot wire, the site is roughly shaped in polystyrene. The model is then finished as before, using filler applied with a spatula.

The site is given its final shape by this process, as well as the desired surface: smooth, rough or variable. If wire mesh is used as a carrier, this is shaped by hand and pinned to the support structure. Instead of using a filler, newspaper or thin cardboard, papier mâché may be employed. Tear up pieces measuring roughly 10×10 cm and soak in wallpaper paste. Paste in several layers on top of the wire mesh matrix, always applying paste to intermediate layers. Allow to dry for at least a day before carrying out further work on the site model. A model made from papier mâché is once again, light and flexible.

6.3 Working with gypsum (Plaster of Paris) models

Gypsum (Plaster of Paris) models are generally only found in competitive tendering situations, when they are supplied by the arbitrators as base standards. The reason for this is that gypsum models are very suitable for series production techniques. They are, however, not worth making if only single models are needed, because they cost too much. One starts with the original model. This has to be rigid and extremely accurate, because all errors and imperfections are carried over onto the casting mould, and thence onto all copies.

Starting with the original model, the negative casting mould is made. A layer of clay, 5–10 mm in thickness, is laid carefully on top of the model, followed by a rigid gypsum mantle. With larger objects this is reinforced with wire mesh or thin steel rods. A suitable cover made from timber battens increases the stability and rigidity of the mould. It makes it easier to position the finished gypsum form shell horizontally to enable other work to proceed. After the gypsum has set, the whole ensemble is turned over and the original model together with the layer of clay is taken out of the gypsum mould. The clay is now stripped from both the original model and the Plaster of Paris mould. Every trace of clay must be removed. Once this has been done, the original model is re-introduced into the mould. The space between it and the Plaster of Paris, which was occupied by the clay, is now filled with silicone rubber solution. Once the rubber has been vulcanized, it is lifted out of the gypsum mould together with the original model, and is separated carefully from it. Because of the elasticity of the rubber, this process is not too difficult. To make copies of the model, the silicone rubber negative is then re-positioned in its original position in the gypsum mantle. It now becomes possible to make as many positive Plaster of Paris copies of the original model as required.

It is important to know how to fit our own design onto the standard gypsum base model. The following fabrication stages are necessary:

– remove buildings which interfere, or are not being taken over
– fit new buildings into the existing ones
– alter parts of the topography (either by raising or reducing levels)
– complete or renew traffic areas
– show correct green areas which accord with the plans
– mark water surfaces

As the position of the new buildings has been fixed, it may be necessary to remove some of the existing buildings. As gypsum models are normally cast as a single entity, i.e. buildings and landscape are one unit, the buildings are simply removed using a chisel. Gypsum can be easily worked provided it has previously been soaked in water. The water can be applied, using a brush or sponge, onto the place where work is to proceed. After the appropriate building components have been removed, the necessary alterations of topography can be carried out. If height layers have to be removed, the appropriate area of gypsum should be well soaked with water. Once the altered positions of the height contours have been transferred from the plans to the model, the new edge of the height contour is cut in with a sharp knife. Using chisels, the superfluous mass is carefully removed. If the surface is damaged in spite of this, it can be repaired with filler applied with a small spatula.

If landscape areas need to be raised, it can be done in two ways. Smaller levels can be applied using filler and a spatula. However if major modifications of land contours or areas are necessary, these are made from cardboard, polystyrene and, if necessary, solid timber. They are then glued to the Plaster of Paris model. Solid timber can only be glued onto dry gypsum, otherwise it gets wet and starts swelling.

Wood is only used for ground floors or other flat building parts. Cardboard and polystyrene are used in appropriate thicknesses to extend height contour layers. The contours of the existing height layers of the model are drawn onto transparent tracing paper, and the new runs of these colour lines are added. Both are then transferred, using a tracing wheel, onto the material used for making the layers, and finally cut out. The

117   Removal of height contour layers from the gypsum casting. The lines drawn are scored, and the excess is cut away.

118   Assembly of height contour layers. Cut either cardboard or polystyrene to the appropriate dimensions and fix on with contact adhesive. Gaps should then be filled neatly with either gypsum or 'Polyfilla', using a spatula. The better the fit of the piece to be inserted, the less extra work (sanding) will be needed. Dry with hot air. Final surface treatment with emulsion paint or very thin gypsum dispersion.

119   The new design is fitted into the site. The green areas are assembled. Drilling into the model to fix tree trunks.

parts are glued on the gypsum model with contact adhesive. Any gaps left are filled carefully with filler. Drying times can be reduced by the use of a hot-air blower. Once the site has been modified to represent the approximate conditions, the new building components are fitted in but not attached. The gypsum model can now be painted. Methods used depend upon whether the design of the existing surroundings should be fitted in, or shown up in a different way. The building sections and the landscape areas are stippled with a water-soluble paint (poster paint, acrylic or emulsion paint). If the design is to be shown separately, the building sections are treated in a different way.

The traffic areas must be positioned before the building components are finally attached. In a gypsum model it is impossible to lift out existing buildings. It is therefore very difficult, or even impossible, to fix masking paper. It is best to cut out streets and squares from white, lightly-toned coloured paper or finely-sprayed thin carton. This can then be attached to the model. It is also possible to use a gouge needle or other tool to provide a different type of texture on traffic areas, green areas and water surfaces. This distinguishes the different areas from each other. Once again, it is essential to work to precise standards because the quality of this work affects the overall impression given by the model.

Once the landscape has been finished, the traffic areas attached, and the buildings fixed on, the green areas can be dealt with. Their character should fit in with the overall concept of the model, quite independently of the nature of the material used, whether natural or artificial.

Trees have trunks. Depending upon the scale of the model, use tooth picks, thin dowels, needles, etc. The crowns of the trees, which are made from a chosen material (see page 112 onwards) are fixed to these. Here, also, it must be mentioned that thoughtful treatment of the layout of the plants affects the overall impression made by the model. The tree trunks must be drilled into the gypsum, as they can otherwise break off easily. Use wood adhesives for gluing, as the residues from such glues neither glisten nor form threads, which can show up badly on photographs. Finally (and sparingly), attach a few scale impression-forming items (people, cars, flag masts, etc.).

120 Building model, 1:50. External walls, roofs, and site area made from 5 mm sandwiched EPS; cut edges glued over. Window areas made from methacrylate sheeting with glued-on 'Letraline' transoms and mullions. The building is erected from basement level (level of base plate). The site adjoins the building.

6.4 The building

With few exceptions, such as topographic models or models depicting plans of green areas to be planted, the building itself is the most important item in architectural model-making. All previous stages of the model-building process, such as construction of base plate, different surface treatment of various parts of the site, etc., have only one purpose: to provide suitable surroundings for the building or groups of buildings and

121 Building model, 1:50. Base plate: 13 mm sandwich timber; site layers: cardboard; building: methacrylate with polystyrene glued onto surface (façade with windows); window profiles made from 'Letraline'; balcony from soldered wire. An internal unit can be seen by lifting off the roof.

to give expression to spatial relationships. Before work is started it is necessary to find out whether all relevant information is to hand. Also, whether all materials and appropriate tools are readily available.

Correct planning of the work demands consideration of the following items:

1 In addition to design drawings, it is a good idea to prepare special information sheets for the model. A photocopier can be used to enlarge or reduce drawings to the scale used in the model

2 How detailed should the model be? This is decided by choosing which aspects are essential to a good understanding of the design. Such aspects include special parts of the building, certain assembly techniques, and the nature of specific shapes

3 The build-up and materials used for fabrication of the model are decided by considering the degree of detailing, the scale, and the model-maker's own method of showing the overall shape of the building

4 Lists of the items needed, additional drawings and test samples of materials should be prepared

5 How is the model of the building to be attached to the base plate? Should it be set onto a flat section of the site, or should the walls go down right to the bottom of the base plate (if the site is mobile)? Under such circumstances the building can be set into a hole in the 'ground'

Fabrication of single parts

As already mentioned, models of buildings can be represented from the architect's point of view as body-, plate- and rod systems, or combinations thereof. When one shapes and fabricates the model of the building, it is essential to be clear about how it should be represented from the outside. Should it be a shaped object, an illustration of how it looks from the inside, or a dialogue between internal and external spaces? These aspects determine how the model is to be built.

122 Fabrication of a stave arrangement. Regular comb-like grooves are cut into a solid rectangular block of wood. These are then cut off in the way shown. The grooves must not be too deep or the rods will be too springy when they are being separated. (*top*)

123 Elongated stave arrangement. Cutting of supported sections of the 'comb' (fig. 122). The small parts can be prevented from getting lost or being sucked up by the vacuum suction plant by gluing a sticky tape over them. (*middle*)

124 Cutting of U and angle profiles. If very small cross-sections are needed, a broad width of the internal side of the profile is cut, which is separated in the final stage of the work. (*bottom*)

125 Mass-production of items by making profiles from maple wood. Using a rectangular timber lath, the cross-section of a chair is produced with various cuts, and the parts are than separated in appropriate lengths. Take stringent safety precautions when carrying out either the lengthwise or the cross cuts! (*above*)

126 Fabrication of holed beams. Operational details. First drill accurate holes into a rectangular timber lath. Using a saw blade 1 mm thick, cut grooves between the holes to half the width of the lath. Separate layers, 1 mm thick, from each other and fix them together. (*above*)

127 Production of arcades from hardwood (maple). Operational details: set out the profiles. The grain runs in the direction of the arcade girders. Mark the centres to be drilled. Drill and cut out residual material between the girders (use a circular-saw). Cut into strips. Position the pieces to make a loadbearing structure. (*below*)

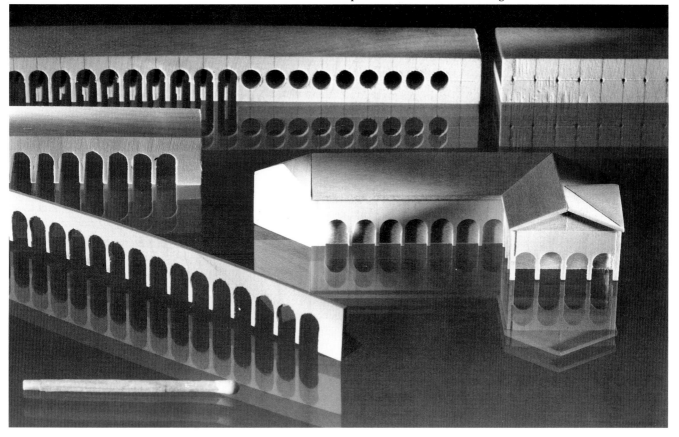

128 Pavilion over the exit from an underground garage. Special model, 1:50. Base plates: 8 mm chipboard doubled up. Road surface and staircase: 3 mm polystyrene. Stanchions: 8 mm methacrylate tubes, containing 4 mm PVC round rods. Holed beams: pear tree wood. Roof surface: scored 0.75 mm thick methacrylate sheeting. Railing: soldered wire.

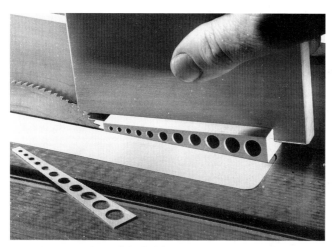

129 Cutting of small holed beams, using a circular-saw. The employment of a push rod of a suitable size enables even small objects to be led safely and accurately past the saw blade.

6.4.1 Rods and profiles

It is possible to buy ready-made rods of wood, polystyrene, aluminium and methacrylate, with round, rectangular and other cross-sections. In addition, small brass profiles with L, T and I cross-sections are readily available. Although there are many different varieties on the market, many rods which are needed for building models need to be specially made for particular purposes. Individual cross-sections and measurements are needed.

The following materials will be used:

1 carton, paper, lined foamed plastic sheeting
2 methacrylate and polystyrene
3 wood: balsa, pear, maple, alder, lime, poplar
4 brass, aluminium, wire

Wooden rods and profiles
A bench circular-saw is required to make these, and in certain cases a bench drilling machine is also required. Please note direction of grain.

6.4.2 Surface areas

The various surface areas are made from the following materials: paper, carton and cardboard; plywood; balsawood, pear, maple, alder, lime or poplar; polystyrene or methacrylate sheeting; brass and aluminium sheeting.

Curved surfaces
Sheets of cardboard, paper-lined expanded polystyrene, solid polystyrene, thin methacrylate or balsa-wood can be bent, but their elastic nature makes them spring back immediately.

To get a permanent curvature, the external surface is scored repeatedly with a knife. The material can then be bent easily along the cuts (fig. 136). In cases where these score marks interfere with the overall effect, glue white or coloured paper over them. If a circular shape, or a sector of it is to be fabricated, first cut out and drill the internal curved section and sand it down. Then continue with the external curved section. Finally, measure and cut out the straight side sections.

Façade surfaces
In the case of building models, the representation of façades is reduced to showing the openings (whether glazed or unglazed), and the closed surfaces (wall elements). Then there are surfaces in front of and behind the level of the walls, and detailed structures (gaps, pillars and ledges). There are also elements which are attached to the façades, such as solar screens, external balconies and staircases, various grilles and gratings.

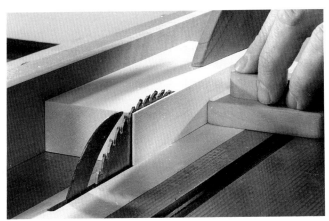

130 Separation of thin discs of hard wood. Thin parts must be able to exit during and after the cutting process. Using the push rod (on top of the block of wood), the work piece is pushed against the saw blade. Only apply this to the back! The wooden guide piece, which is held by the visible hand, presses the piece of wood in front of the saw blade against the lengthwise guide.

131 Cutting of a grille structure. A thin sheet of hardwood is closely slotted on both sides, but turned through an angle of 90°. The depth of cuts is more than half the thickness of the wood.

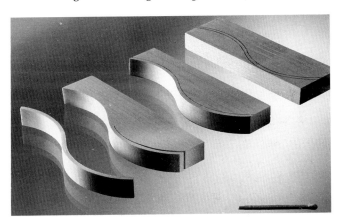

132 Cutting curved pieces from solid maple wood. Steps of carrying out work: trace contours onto piece of wood. Cut out one side of shape and sand down. Cut out and sand other side. It is always best to ensure that small parts are completely finished before separating them from a larger piece of wood. (*left*)

133 Rings made from solid timber. Steps of carrying out work: set up the piece on the drilling table. Drill out central hole, and sand the surface. Cut out the approximate external circle and equalize by sanding, using the plate grinding machine. (*below*)

When a model façade structure is being developed, it is not only necessary to consider its scale and the degree of detailing needed. It is also important to regard the façade surfaces together, as an overall exercise in spatial design. In this respect we not only have to consider the proportions of single surface areas, but also the ratio of the various surfaces and parts of surfaces to each other. Their positions are as important in this respect as their shapes.

Is the surface horizontal or vertical? What are the size, shape, and directional contrasts? What material contrasts (metal, polystyrene, cardboard, etc.) are there? What are the surface contrasts (shiny, plain, smooth, rough, grained, hatched, etc.)? Are there light/dark or colour contrasts?

We have to decide which contrasts we will adopt and how they are to be shown in the building model in order to obtain the desired overall effect. Depending upon the methods of construction employed, the following techniques are used to represent the façade areas:

1 The elevations, which have previously been drawn and, if so desired, painted, are glued onto the carrier structure. In simple models, tracings can be taken from the design drawings.

2 A more natural representation is obtained if façade photographs are taken of existing buildings. These are then enlarged according to the scale used, duplicated and glued on to the building structure. Additional effects can be obtained using squared paper,

134 Façade section, 1:25. Loadbearing framework from 8 mm chipboard. Façade areas: 3 mm methacrylate sheeting. Rounded section from 100 mm diameter methacrylate tubing, which was cut into four pieces. Closed surfaces at the back are sprayed grey. Facing sections: 1 mm grooves were cut out with a circular-saw, and attached on both sides with 'Letraline' glue. Window-cleaning balconies are made from 1 mm thick polystyrene, with wire fly screen laid on. PVC round rods, 2 mm diameter, are also used. (below)

135 Façade model, 1:50. Loadbearing part: 5 mm sandwiched EPS. Façades: structured polystyrene 1 mm thick; frame sections: 'Letraline', grey coloured paper; supports made from hardwood. Vertical curtains and roof overhangs: 2 or 3 mm thick polystyrene. Frieze made from grooved hardwood, 1.5 mm methacrylate sheeting with scored and coloured glass building brick structure. Window frames: 'Tetraline'. Grey paper is laid at the back of windows and glass building bricks to make the design stand out. Scaffolding from soldered wire. All surface connections are facilitated using double-sided adhesive foil. (right)

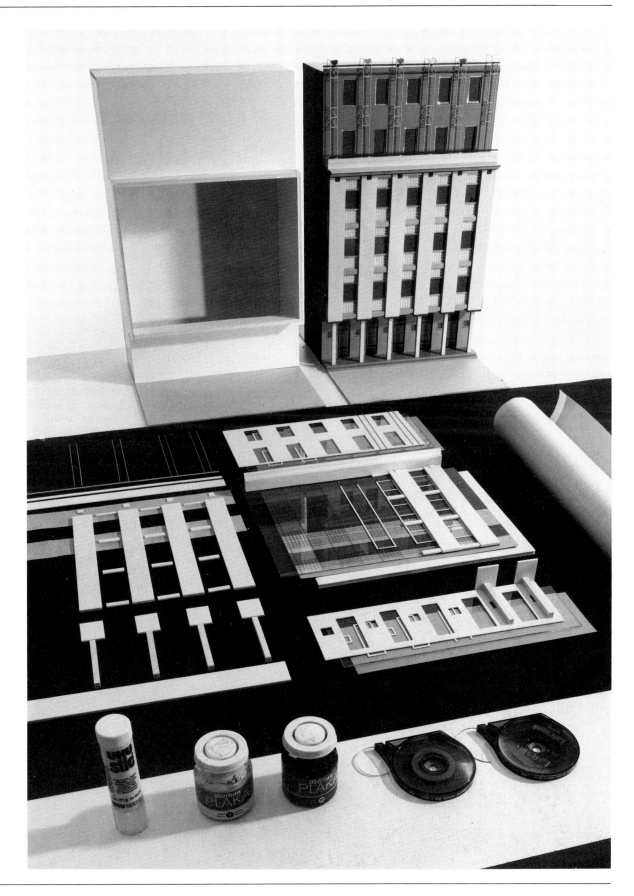

coloured papers, or even a spray-gun. Such photographic façades can be cut up and reassembled as reliefs at various heights.

3 A collage made up from different materials is assembled, which can be cut and glued onto the façade surface in any way desired.

4 The solid building structure can also be treated directly by drawing and painting.

5 The surface of a solid building structure can be cut, punched, scored, etc., and various profiles and shapes can be glued on. In this way the surface areas of the model building can be shaped directly to form the various façade walls.

6 The façade can be made as an individual surface area.

Both single-layer and multiple-layer-type façades can be fabricated as panels. Once completed, each panel can either be attached to a carrier frame, or it may be self-loadbearing. The façade panels thereby form the external skin of the building.

136 Curved walls can be made from methacrylate sheeting, which has been bent by a hot-air blower against a template. Methacrylate sheeting, which is either 0.8 mm or 1 mm thick, can be scored and bent carefully along the score marks. Wire mesh, perforated sheeting and corrugated cardboard can be shaped more easily. Cardboard and sandwiched EPS are best cut on the convex side of the bend.

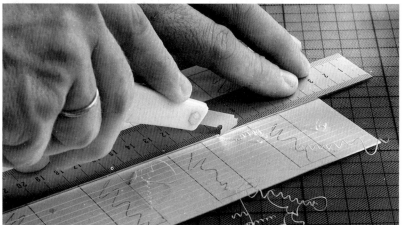

137 Scoring and grooving. A hooked blade is excellent for scoring polystyrene and methacrylate sheeting, to enable them to be structured, or to prepare them for making a clean break. To break the sheet, the cut is first of all deepened by using a normal sharp knife blade.
Take care not to cut down to the cutting surface with the hooked knife blade.

138 If one wishes to obtain precise cuts in paper, cardboard, polystyrene or methacrylate sheeting, it is essential to use a new, sharp blade, an undamaged steel ruler, and a good cutting surface.

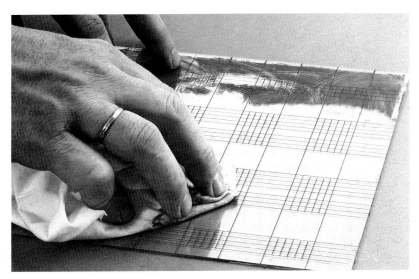

139 A structure which has been scored using a hooked blade is accentuated by rubbing in water-soluble pigmented paint. Use a soft cloth which does not leave loose threads. Allow to dry, and then polish clean. The pigment remains in the score marks, while the surfaces stay bright.

140 Methacrylate and polystyrene are best joined by low-viscosity solvents. The parts to be joined must fit together exactly. Using a watercolour paintbrush, apply the solvent along the joint. The surface to be glued is softened slightly, and the parts are 'welded' together. In our experience it is best to use a brush rather than an injection needle. The exact dose is difficult to determine and apply.

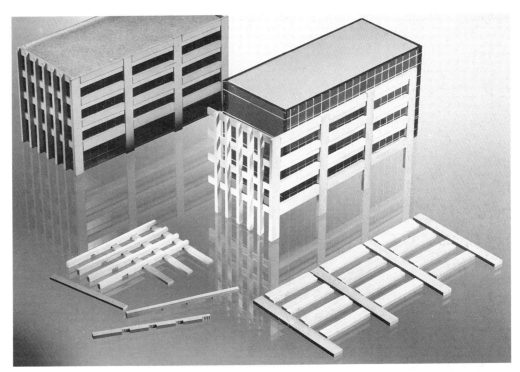

142 Building model, 1:200. Loadbearing structure (no soffit on inside): dark-coloured methacrylate sheeting with score marks coloured white. Stanchions and beams: sawn pear wood. (*above*)

143 Building model, 1:200. Loadbearing structure: 3 mm grey polystyrene, sprayed grey in cloud shapes. Exchangeable variants of façades made from coloured methacrylate sheeting, which is sprayed, then scored with design details engraved on the surface. (*below*)

141 Façade with windows, 1:50. With such large-scale façades it is possible, instead of using a complete sheet of methacrylate, to employ frames, either with or without 'panes'. Façade: 10 mm sandwiched EPS; window openings: cut with modelling knife, cut edges covered by glued strips. Ground floor: no frame. First-floor frame soldered from 1×3 mm brass profiles. Second-floor frame soldered from 1.2 mm wire. Third-floor panes from 1 mm methacrylate sheeting; frame: 'Tetraline'. (*left*)

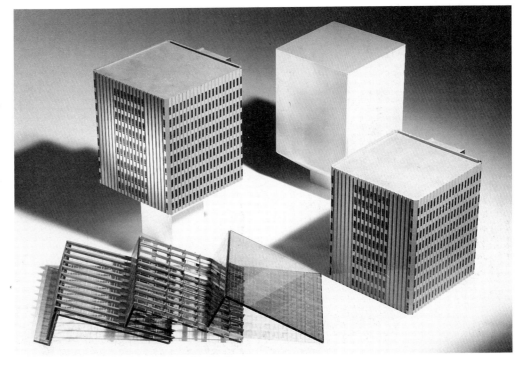

Single-layer façade areas can be cut from methacrylate sheeting, polystyrene, brass or aluminium sheeting. By scoring the sheet with a hooked knife blade or similar, it is possible to mark finer details such as window profiles, stone joints, etc. Paints can be rubbed into these scratch marks (see above) to accentuate them. The sur-faces can also be painted with a spray-gun, using masking paper to protect other sections (Section 6.2.5).

Façade areas which are built up in several layers often use a base of methacrylate sheeting which is cut to the size of a whole wall. The solid wall components (sections made from polystyrene, wood and cardboard),

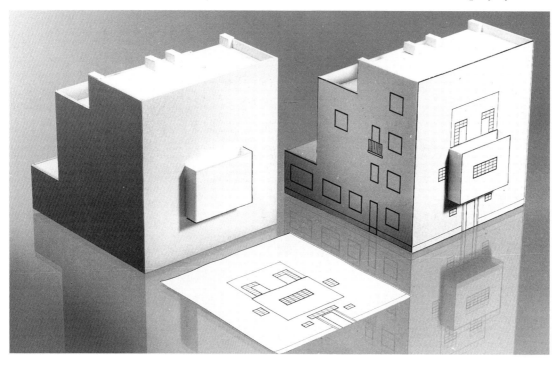

144 Building model, 1:100. Building constructed from 1.5 mm cardboard.
Left: The building as a solid shape.
Right: Copies of the plan glued on to form façade. (*above*)

145 Building model, 1:100 as fig. 144.
Left: window areas formed by backing with coloured paper; 1 mm carton used as façade.
Right: window areas only shown in relief. (*below*)

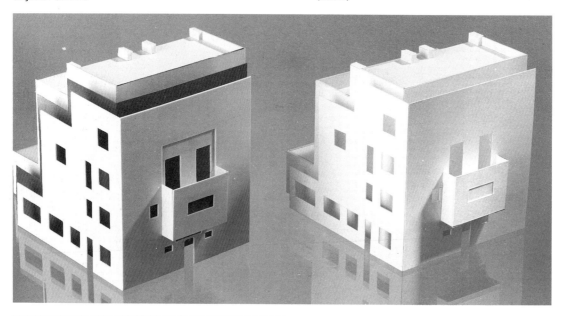

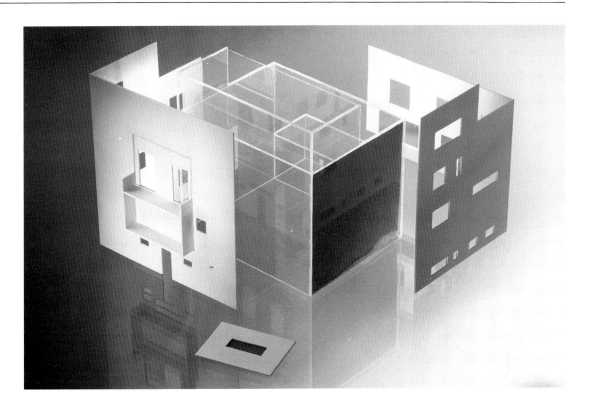

146 Building model, 1:100. Core structure
made from 1.5 mm methacrylate sheeting with
grey paper glued to the back. Window façade
from 1 mm polystyrene, with double-sided
adhesive foil stuck to surface. (*above*)

147 Building model, 1:100. Made in the same
way as shown in Fig. 146, but with scored
and coloured window mullions and transoms.
Balcony railings: soldered wires. (*below*)

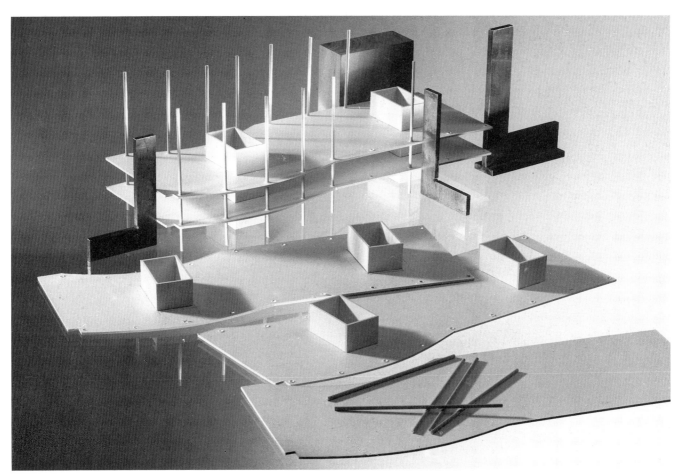

148　How to construct a building model, 1:200, for interior inspection. Floor soffits and building cores (distance pieces): 1.5 mm cardboard. Stanchions: 2mm PVC round rods. Assembly using angle piece templates.

149　Façade variants for loadbearing structure shown in fig. 148.
Left: Glass façade made from 1 mm methacrylate sheeting, which has been scored and bent. Right: Façade structure made from soldered wire. The elements can also be combined. Glazing can be set separately for each floor, behind the stanchions (not shown in the illustration).

which have already had windows and door openings cut out, are pasted onto their fronts. The acrylic sheeting then looks like glass windows. Further effects can be achieved by application of coloured paper, mirror foil or coloured foils. Mullions and transoms can either be scored and painted in, or represented by pasting on small strips. To make such adhesive strips yourself, stick some coloured paper or carton onto double-sided adhesive foil, and cut into thin strips.

Roofs and terraces
Roof and terrace areas must not be neglected. After all, most models are looked at from the top, and therefore such areas stand out. Here, too, a decision needs to be made whether roofs should be expressed in a natural or abstract form, by making a choice of specific colours and structures. Always think of the scale and how all the different parts of the model act together. If the scale of the model is small, the roof surfaces are usually left untreated.

The following materials are considered:

– coloured, treated corrugated cardboard (particularly the very fine micro-corrugated cardboard)
– scored polystyrene or methacrylate sheeting

150 Various materials and structures used for the construction of roofs. Roof tiles made from polystyrene, scored and sprayed. Trapezium-shaped metal sheet: micro-corrugated cardboard or finely ribbed rubber flooring sheeting. Bituminous roof: cork sheeting, either stained or sprayed. Metal sheet roofing: thin aluminium or copper sheet, in some cases with profiles. Tent roof: ladies' stockings. Gravel roof: sandpaper with various grain sizes. Plate roofs: polystyrene, scored with a hooked knife blade. Pergolas: wire mesh.

– sandpaper using different grain sizes (in some cases coloured sandpaper)
– various decorative papers
– brass, copper or aluminium sheeting
– offset sheets
– other materials

6.4.3 Solid structures

Building components can be produced as solid bodies, or they can be hollow. They can also be represented as vertical sections, or by horizontal layers. (Continued on page 98)

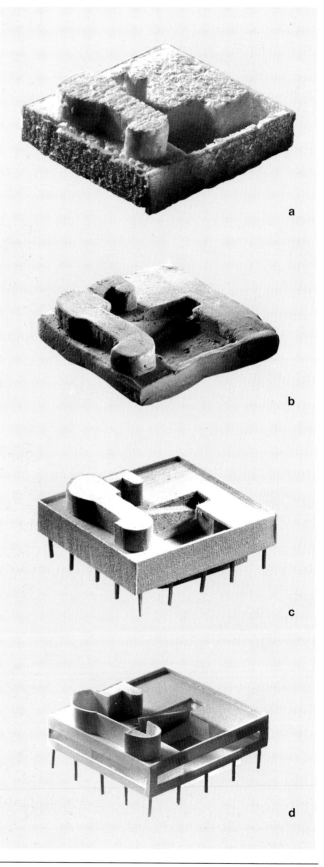

151 Building model, 1:500. Base plate: 5 mm thick black methacrylate sheeting. Building made from transparent and black methacrylate sheet. Adjoining core structures: matt sanded methacrylate. Façades: methacrylate with scored-in features. (*above*)

152 Building model. (*right*)
a. Conceptual model constructed from expanded polystyrene
b. Conceptual model made from clay
c. Work model made from lime wood
d. Exhibition model using methacrylate, polystyrene, wire
   (Illustrations are actual size)

The four illustrations on this page show how many different methods are available to represent a building with scale 1:500. These range from 'solid blocks' to 'merely indicative'. The builder of the model must make his or her own decision regarding the amount of detailing to be used for each specific scale.

153 Building models, 1:500.
Left: solid. Centre: solid with openings punched in. Right: solid, with recessed bottom and top edges.

154 Building models, 1:500.
Left: structured horizontally. Centre: structured vertically. Right: structured both horizontally and vertically.

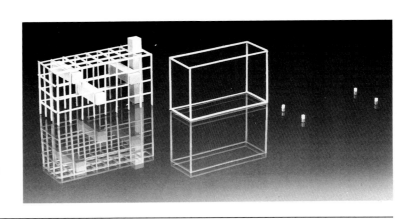

155 Building models, 1:500.
Left: expressed as planes which are carried by a central core. Centre: expressed as planes which are supported by side cores. Right: expressed as a collection of horizontal and vertical planes (floor and wall units).

156 Building models, 1:500.
Left: space lattices made from rods, with surfaces and solid bodies enclosed. Centre: edges of solid bodies. Right: the corners are supported by feet.

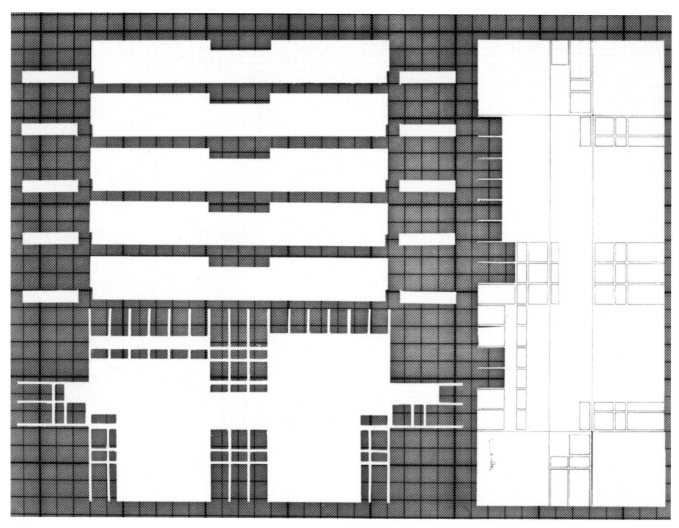

157–159 Development of a building model, scale 1:500,
using white photographic carton.
Stages of operation:
– Tracing of correctly-dimensioned roof and wall areas;
  cutting them out.
– Scoring of edges of building to enable them to be turned
  over.
– Flooring sections and distance pieces are drawn, cut out
  and glued together to form a loadbearing model.
– Covering the loadbearing model with the external skin,
  and gluing the whole together, using great care.

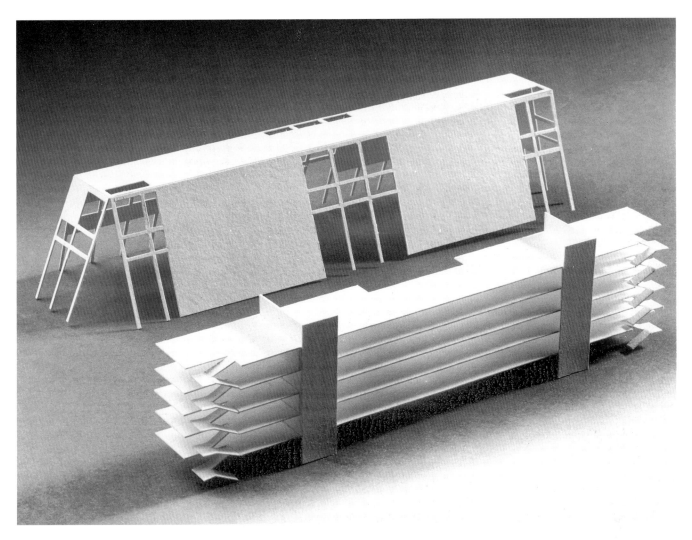

160 When cutting small parts lengthwise, a push rod is used to lead them evenly past the saw blade. The push rod must fit exactly.

When cutting the correct lengths, the parts must be able to fall off at the side. This is the reason why the side guide is equipped with a wooden distance block, with which the lengths to be cut off can be measured. This distance block must be positioned well in front of the saw blade.

 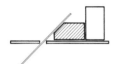 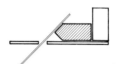

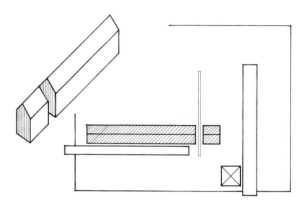

162 Cutting the profile of a building. Method used: first cut the two slanting roofs, and then cut correct lengths.

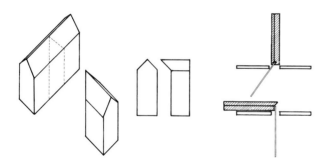 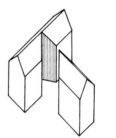 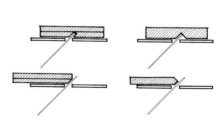

163 Procedure for cutting out buildings.
Left: preparation with cut-out roof sections
Right: all building sections mitred together

164 Solid building being fitted together – compare fig. 163.
Left: Cut-out roof section.
Right: Mitred section.

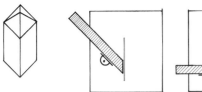

165 Procedure for cutting small parts: cut the shape from all sides and only separate off right at the end.

166 The finished cut roof pyramid (hipped roof) is only cut away when completely finished.

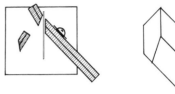

167 Cutting scheme for angled buildings.

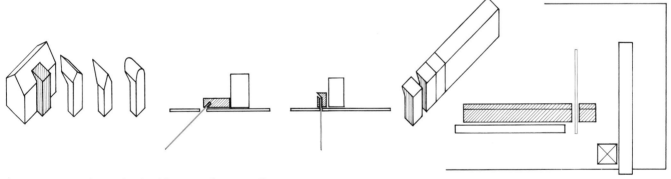

168 Cutting scheme for buildings with protruding sections.

169 The profile of a roof window is separated off and sanded to fit in with the roof shape.

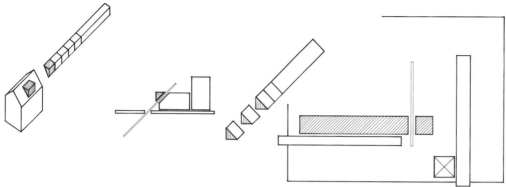

170 Cutting scheme for 1:500 roof window sections and similar very small parts.

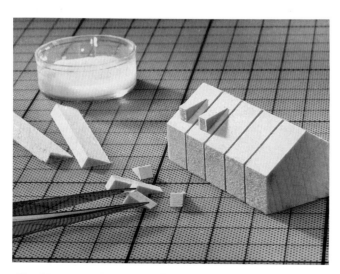

172 Using woodworker's adhesive to glue a roof window section on. Tweezers are needed to hold the part in position.

173 Urban model, 1:500. Base plate: 10 mm chipboard. Height contour layers: 2 mm cork. Different surface areas: sprayed. Buildings made from maple wood. All parts are cut out by means of a circular-saw.

174 Flat grooves mark the single houses. A spare block of wood is placed behind the cell of houses, to lead the part to be cut safely, and to prevent the single houses from jamming, once they have been cut off. (*top*)

175 The separate parts for a larger building complex, 1:500. The model-maker has to reduce the whole to single components in such a way that he or she can then rebuild it from these parts. (*middle*)

176 The complex as shown in fig. 175, and the way it is built up. The base plate consists of 10 mm chipboard. Traffic and green areas are represented in relief using 1 mm photographic carton. Parts of the buildings are made from poplar wood. Trees are made from pieces of a bathroom loofah. (*bottom*)

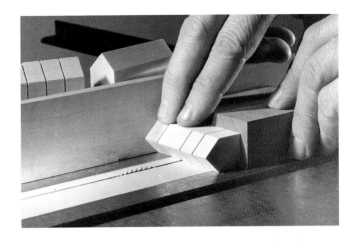

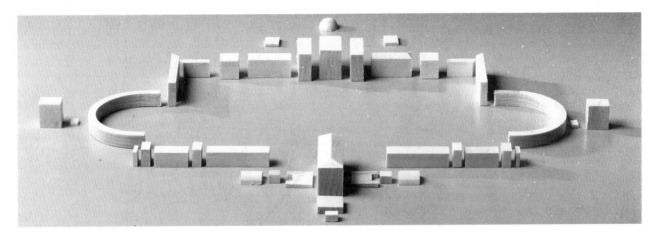

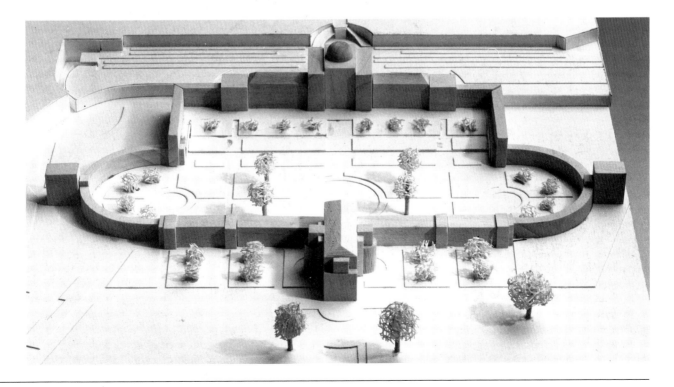

Massive structures can be cut, using a thermal-saw, from foamed plastics, or shaped from 'Plasticine', clay, gypsum or timber. Larger items are best constructed from sheets of cardboard, paper-lined expanded polystyrene or plywood, and rather less often, from metal sheeting. The hollow core saves material and weight. A tall building appears to be lighter if assembled from horizontal plates held together by a central core. This type of building may be covered by façade surfaces.

6.4.4 Soldered structures

Soldering techniques have become more popular in the field of architectural model-building, during the last few years. The tools necessary are not expensive and are readily available. A soldering kit (soldering iron plus accessories) takes little room, and it is easy to learn how to use the equipment.

It is easy and quick to make technical objects, sections of buildings or even whole buildings entirely by means of a soldering iron, solder, wires and metal sheeting. The only tools needed are simple ones such as pliers, clamps and tweezers. The resulting models are good to look at, without being 'over the top'. They appeal to the viewer because of their accuracy, lightness and transparency. Many models achieve the character of expensive jewellery. In many ways, soldering is better than other methods of fabrication. A soldered building structure gives a better insight into the way a building is to be shaped than one which is made from methacrylate sheeting or glued together from wooden strips, without in any way being less attractive. Using soft soldering for architectural model construction is much easier than would appear. Yet the finished article has an excellent appearance.

Materials and equipment necessary for soldering
A soldering iron with a fine tip and a minimum thermal output of 40 watts is needed. If a lot of soldering is carried out, it is best to acquire a special soldering bench kit, with a thermostat and several exchangeable soldering tips. Small gas-fired soldering irons, which operate independently of a mains circuit and do not have trailing flexes, give excellent service. To join two metal surfaces it is necessary to use solder. Solder is available in the form of rods, wire or as a ready fluxed wires. To get a clean, strong and barely visible soldering joint flux must be used. Fluxes are available in the form of solutions, oils and fats. All three prevent the oxidation of the heated base metal, and therefore allow the surface to be wetted by the molten solder.

The main materials used for building architectural models are galvanized and flexible steel wire of between 0.3 mm and 1.5 mm thick. In addition, all kinds of brass wires and rods, as well as brass sheeting and profiles and thin iron rods, are eminently suitable for soldering purposes.

The following are unsuitable for soldering: flower wire, spring steel and aluminium. Auxiliary equipment, needed both for preparing the various items and for the actual soldering, includes a good pair of shears or a flat pair of pliers with a cutter on the side. One or more pairs of tweezers are also needed, if possible with an insulated handle to protect the user's hands. The various items are fixed onto a paper template with either masking tape or double-sided 'Sellotape'. Alternatively, they can be laid into a wooden or cardboard template, a method which is particularly advantageous when many similar elements have to be fabricated. Both hands are now free. One is used to hold the soldering iron and to position it accurately, whilst the other holds the various parts in position with tweezers, or applies flux and solder.

177   Lift tower, 1:50. All parts are made from 5×1 mm brass tubing. Bracing with 1 mm brass wire. Gas soldering irons reach a high temperature, and there should be no cable to interfere.

The vital consideration with the entire technique of soldering is that both metal parts are heated sufficiently well at the joint that the solder is able to flow into it. It is not the liquid solder on the surface of the soldering iron which guarantees a firm joint, but the heated metal parts, between which the hot solder is able to flow. Thin metal sections heat up very quickly. There is always the danger when soldered layers lie close to each other that joints which have already been made can come apart again. This can be prevented by conducting the heat away, using clamps or other pieces of metal. Alternatively, the parts which have already been

178 Items needed for soldering: water-resistant felt pen, pair of pliers/cutters, metal saw, various thicknesses of wire, calibrated metal ruler, metal profiles, tweezers, soldering paste, solder, various types of fluxes, crêpe paper masking tape, soldering-iron.

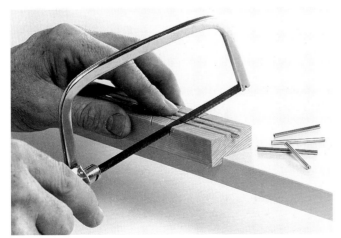

179 Cutting correct lengths of brass profile with a metal saw using a home-made grooved template lath.

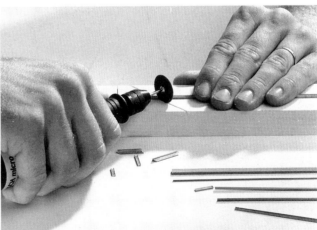

180 Using a small revolving cutting disk it is easy to cut the correct lengths of profiles, either at right angles or at a slant. Always wear safety glasses!

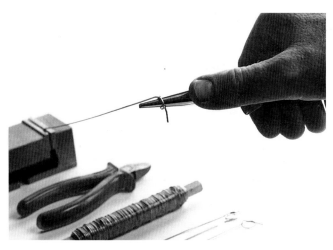

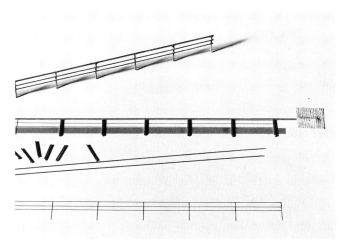

181 Wire with diameters between 0.2 and 1.2 mm is used. This must always be stretched prior to soldering.

182 Railings made from stretched wire. The drawing is shown at the bottom. In the centre, the components are fixed in position on top of an adhesive tape prior to soldering. The upper illustration shows the finished railings.

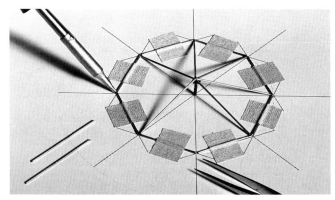

183 Brass capsules are pushed into nails which have been set into pre-drilled holes of the octagonal base design.

184 The upper corona is made by means of an auxiliary plate. A nail is used in the centre as a support, and horizontal parts are attached with crêpe paper masking tape prior to soldering.

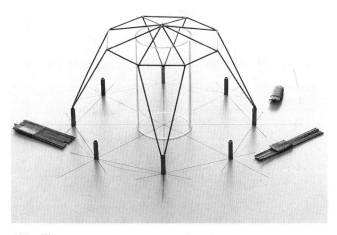

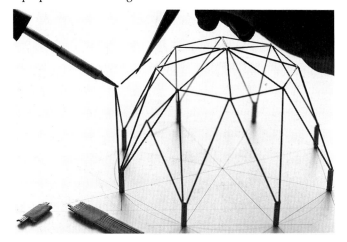

185 The upper corona is now placed on top of a piece of methacrylate tubing of the correct height. The connecting rods between the upper corona and the brass capsules are soldered into position.

186 The missing rods are next held and soldered into position.

soldered can be supported with masking tape. When three-dimensional structures are soldered, the matter is somewhat more difficult. It is best to use an auxiliary

construction, made from cardboard tubes, cardboard sheeting and wooden blocks: all materials able to withstand short-term heat. The pieces which are to be soldered can then be fixed reasonably firmly and soldered.

The overall aim is always to get almost invisible soldered joints which satisfy the high standards set for architects' models and simulation techniques. Landscapes, carriers and other formations with bends and corners can be soldered horizontally. They can then be shaped afterwards. Soldering can only be carried out if the components to be soldered are not too thick.

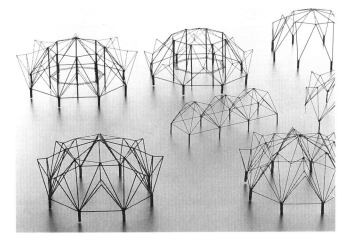

187 Preliminary studies regarding ultimate shape. The design is developed and optimized on the model, not the drawings.

188 The final exhibition model. The lattice structure is made from stretched wire. The entire metal structure is nickel-coated by a specialist firm. All areas are covered with 0.8 mm methacrylate foil. Palms are made from finely-cut aluminium foil.

189 Designs of a large entry portal, 1:33. The wall unit consists of chipboard, coated and structured with polystyrene. Soldered items are made from brass wire, stretched iron wire, brass sheeting, galvanized sheeting, and fly mesh. (*left*)

190 Soldering template for one of the door designs described in fig. 189. All parts are positioned on a strip of crêpe paper masking tape. (*below*)

7 Worked Examples

The fabrication of building structures is shown here in the form of actual examples. In contrast to the building of the base plate and site models, each model of a building requires a special technique. The designs featured are only examples of what can be done.

191 Medical faculty, Göttingen. Complete layout, 1:1000. Base plate: 13 mm chipboard. Height contour layers: 1 mm cork. All buildings made from balsa-wood, cut with a circular-saw.

Dormitories (*right*): horizontal layers. Examination and treatment block (*centre*): horizontal layers with vertical supports. Roof has air-conditioning units with streaked vertical mounts. Administration centre (*left*): horizontal layers fronted by access towers. The direction of the grain is intentionally used to differentiate between the divisions. The colours of all the elements are chosen to blend with each other, and the different areas (vehicle, traffic, parking, pedestrian, etc.) are indicated by colouring them with spray paint. Trees: lambswool.

Note the high level of detail for the scale of 1:1000, which nevertheless manages to avoid overcomplicating the model.

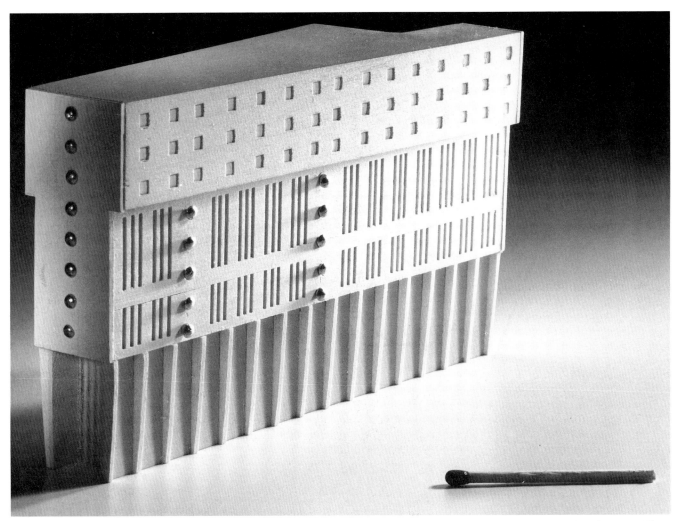

192 Building model, 1:500. Maple wood, circular-saw, sanding machine. The three layers were fabricated separately. Base: solid block. Vertical girders glued on and ground at a slant. Central part: solid block. Using a saw blade 1.6 mm wide, the vertical window slits of both frontages are cut into like a comb. Intermediate parts are made from laths which have been accurately cut and glued on. Nickel-coated ornamental nails. Upper floor: solid block with window openings chiselled out. The central and upper parts of both end elevations bear glued-on thin plates.

These two models have the same scale of 1:500. They act totally different from each other because of their contrasting construction materials, namely wood and plastics. The closed building above exhibits the normal picture of a closed body. In contrast, the one opposite shows a totally open design. It also allows inspection of internal features.

193 Building model, 1:500. Base plate used as assembly slab: 16 mm chipboard. Traffic and green areas represented as a relief by means of 0.75 mm polystyrene sheeting. Before the areas are cut out, sticky foil is attached to the back and glued onto the chipboard, which is completely covered with polystyrene.

All building components are made from 1 mm polystyrene and methacrylate sheeting. The pieces are partly sawn, and partly cut out with a knife. All polystyrene parts are sprayed matt white before being glued together. Trees are made from 8 mm diameter methacrylate rods, sanded matt, with drilled-in trunks made from 2 mm diameter methacrylate rods. It is unusual to show internal rooms with 1:500 building models. The model-maker's intention was to clearly indicate the basic concept of the museum, as well as its two sections.

194   Building model, 1:200. Base plate: 16 mm sandwiched timber. Streets shown in relief using 0.7 mm polystyrene. Loadbearing frame as sectioned cube, 3 mm sandwiched EPS. Façades: continuous 0.8 mm methacrylate foil. Divisions scored in with hooked knife blade and coloured black.
Foil is sprayed grey at the back and fixed fully with double-sided adhesive foil. Parapets and vertical cladding were made from 0.5 mm polystyrene and fixed against the methacrylate using double-sided adhesive foil. Railings, flag poles, etc.: made from stretched and soldered wire. Existing buildings: 1 mm methacrylate sheeting. The restrained character of the existing buildings accentuates the architectural qualities of the design. Virtually the entire model was made by hand, without the use of any machinery. (*top left*)

195   Building model, 1:200. Base plate: 16 mm sandwiched timber slab measuring 55×85 cm. Water surface: ornamental glass with coloured paper underneath. Site and building construction from layered thick carton. Some elements: soldered fine wires. Aluminium tubes. Round metal rods. Combination of surfaces and rods. Walls and ceilings can be partly removed. This permits inspection of the internal layout of the concert hall, and examination of the correlation between the inside and the outside of the buildings. (*bottom left*)

196–198   Building model, 1:100, which has been taken apart floor by floor. 1 mm polystyrene, 0.8 mm methacrylate foil, 2 mm diameter PVC round rods. All parts have been cut out with a hooked blade or a modelling knife and joined by means of a solvent adhesive.

The curved wall elements on the flat roofs are polystyrene strips, which were bent round some piping until they formed the desired shape without springing back.

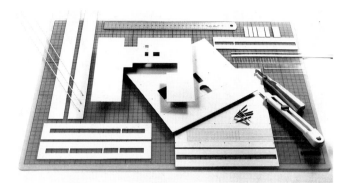

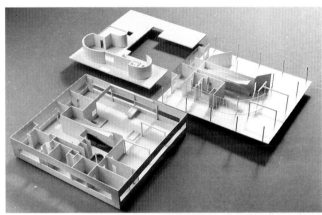

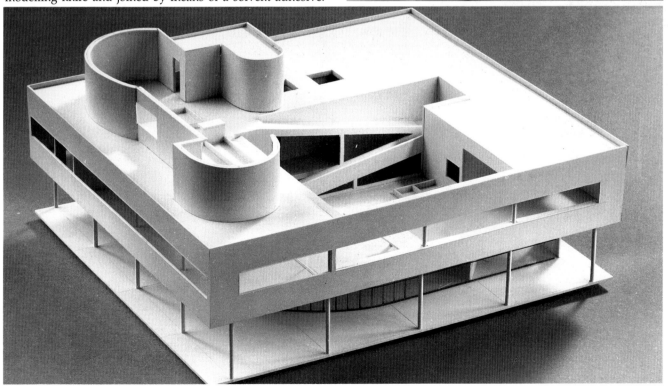

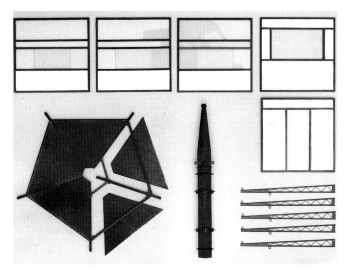

199–201   Model of a kiosk, 1:20.

199   The building elements of the façades and roof. Façade elements are made from 1.5 mm methacrylate sheeting, which is covered with white carton. The timber-framing components are painted in. The parts used for construction are hardwood or brass profiles. (*top*)

200   The internal parts. Wall elements are made in the same way as the external façades. The suspended roof is made from white cardboard, covered with veneers. Internal fittings: polystyrene. All parts are painted. (*middle*)

201   The fine details exhibited by the complete model. The colours and various materials can also be seen clearly. (*bottom*)

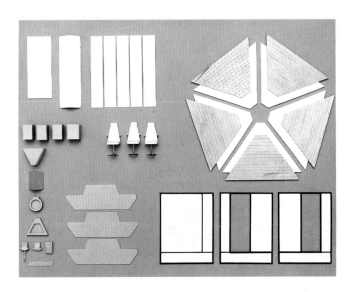

202   Internal room model, 1:50. Section though foyer, auditorium and stage. Length: about 2.4 metres, capable of being dismantled into three sections. Soffits, wall elements and other constructional parts are made from 2.5 mm thick grey cardboard. Visible areas are covered with coloured paper. Furnishing and figures are indicated with cardboard.
This sectional model is excellent in showing the relationship of the various areas to each other. It also clearly indicates concepts regarding colours and materials. The only tools needed for making this model were a steel ruler, a set-square and a universal modelling knife. (*top right*)

203   Stage set: 1:50. Base plate: 19 mm sandwiched timber slab. Flooring in steps: plywood. Different surfaces shown by veneers, coloured papers, sandpaper, emery paper. Cranes and ancillary structures made from glued cardboard or soldered metal rods. Bath tubs, toilets, etc. made from cast gypsum. Furniture: hardwood. Changing cabins: coloured cardboard. The model gives a very realistic impression of the intended effect. (*bottom right*)

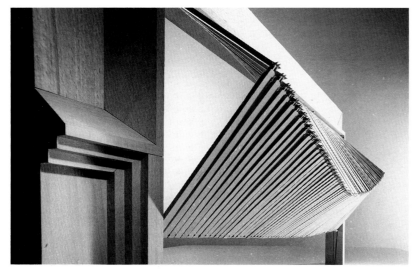

204   Portal, 1:20. Vertically closing door. Staves of beech wood.

205–209   School pavilion. Construction model, 1:33. All parts were cut on the circular-saw from pear wood. This model was the main object used as a basis for discussions between the various building engineers, carpenters, and the developer.

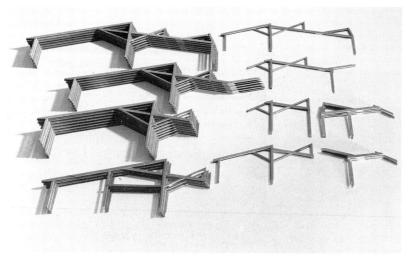

205   The parts are positioned accurately onto an assembly template.

206   All trusses for the circular building structure have been prepared.

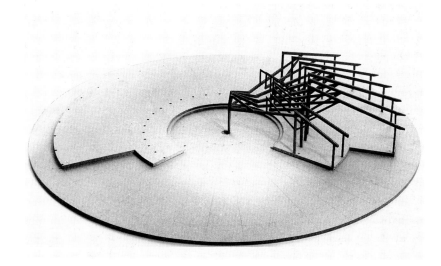

207 Simulated order of work for erection of trusses.

208 Bird's-eye view of the actual building site. Model-builders and carpenters work according to similar principles.

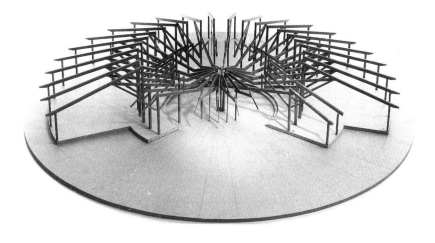

209 The structure after erection.

8 Materials Used to Indicate Scale

The purpose of such materials is to give the viewer an idea of the scale of the model and its component parts. We can relate the model to reality, and are helped to 'read' its true dimensions. The designer also benefits, in that it becomes possible to investigate the ratios of sizes chosen directly, on the model. Some parts of the model are used right from the start to clarify the scale employed: subdivision of windows, window profiles, staircases, hand rails, fencing, supports, an accurate representation of existing structures and details etc.

The addition of scale impression-forming items, such as trees, vehicles and figures, changes the character of the model. On the one hand, it can strengthen the intended naturalistic character. One the other, it can accentuate the abstract nature of the building as against the scale impression items. The use of such items, with their leaning towards realism, is always a step towards naturalistic model building. It is therefore important for us to decide how far we should go in using such items, without spoiling the effect we aim at in the first place. It is easy for an internal model which has been furnished very fully and accurately to become a mere doll's house. Brightly-painted trees on green sawdust can result in a kitsch, rather than a naturalistic effect.

Two groups of scale impression-forming items are distinguishable:

1 Items which are directly connected to the building model and make it seem more detailed. The following may belong to this category:

- components of a vertical nature, such as staircases, ramps, ladders, railings and hand rails
- window features, such as transoms, mullions and frame sections
- profiles for beams and stanchions, made from brass or timber
- furnishing of internal rooms such as wardrobes, tables, stools, chairs, mobile wall units, glass cabinets and cupboards
- more rarely, human figures

2 Items which only perform an auxiliary function with respect to the building and are added merely as an afterthought. These describe the surrounding area of the building, and encourage the viewer to look at the building more closely. The most important are:

- trees and bushes
- human figures
- vehicles, aircraft, boats
- urban features (benches, telephone kiosks, bus stops)
- street lights (street lamps, beacons etc.)
- railings, fences

All these components can be made by do-it-yourself methods. Many semi-finished products are obtainable from model-making firms, or from specialist shops for electronic components, dressmaking, horticulture, laboratory equipment, etc. If we want to make figures, vehicles or furniture from timber profiles, it is best to choose timber with a dense and neutral structure such as poplar, maple, alder, lime or pear.

Often it may be important to acquire properly painted and shaped objects, when neither the time or tools are available to make them. It is then possible to purchase what is needed in shops specializing in supplying model-makers. They stock finished trees, figures, vehicles, railings, fences, etc. in various different scale modifications. Take care, however: model railways and other similar models usually work to different scales. Only buy such parts from them, where the size tends to vary (for example, trees). Finished components which do correspond to the scale dimensions required can be bought from specialist shops. However, they generally need to be ordered in advance from a catalogue. If the model is to be photographed, it is best not to glue trees and other additional items on too firmly. They can then be moved if they interfere with the photograph.

210 Scale-indicating items. The parts are required in many different scale sizes. Components needed are not only people, animals, cars and aircraft, but also staircases, railings, furniture, flagpoles and many other items.

8.1 Trees and bushes

It is very seldom that one finds an architectural model without trees. Yet nothing can, quite unintentionally, give such a wrong impression of the scale of the model as the incorrect choice of dimensions of these items. If a tree is too low, or the diameter of the top is too small, the building appears to be higher and more massive. It is also important that the trees are positioned in the right places. Depending upon where they are placed, it is possible to emphasize directions, spaces and characteristics which accord with the ideas of our design. Trees and bushes should never be scattered all over the place, even if this is realistically accurate. It is also a bad idea to mix different methods of representation (for example, wooden balls and sheep's wool). Always try to show trees as possessing trunks, even if the scale is 1:500. Such a representation gives the viewer something to look through, without blocking off the building, which is of great importance for the model. Before finally placing the trees in the model, check their effect. Simulate the position with pieces of screwed-up paper, and try to produce a single entity from the trees, buildings and surroundings. Try not to overdo things.

There are numerous ways of representing trees and bushes. Before starting, it is best to look carefully at trees in their natural state, and to photograph them for the materials collection. Specific types of growth can then be examined, and incorporated in the model. It is advisable to establish a collection of samples of home-made trees using various techniques and scales. It will soon become clear that a model tree cannot be made in five minutes. The green areas of the model should also not be left to the last minute if high quality standards and effectiveness are to be achieved.

The choice of the shape of trees and bushes not only depends upon the scale of measurement of the model, but also on the overall impression the final model should make. The aim is to show the tree true to scale in its overall shape, and not just as a particular species. Fundamentally, the shape of a tree may resemble a sphere, a cone, a cylinder or an umbrella.

Trees made from naturally-occurring materials
Cones from fir trees, pines or larch can be used. Small twigs which have a lot of joints, dried azaleas, bits of sheep's wool and various umbels are also employed. Walks in the countryside will provide inspiration. It may be necessary to re-shape the found objects slightly, but they will at least appear in the model in their natural forms.

Other natural products, such as Iceland moss, a bathroom loofah or sponge, can serve as raw materials from

Actual size of fully-grown trees	Size in model		
Height (m)	1:20 (cm) 1:200 (mm)	1:50 (cm) 1:500 (mm)	1:100 (cm) 1:1000 (mm)
Sequoia tree up to 100	500	200	100
Douglas fir 50–60	250–300	100–120	50–60
Fir, Pine or Deal 30–40	150–200	60–80	30–40
Yew tree, Thuja 10–15	50–75	20–30	10–15
Beech, Elm 30–40	150–200	60–80	30–40
Oak, Poplar 25–35	125–175	50–70	25–35
Maple, Lime, Plane tree 20–30	100–150	40–60	20–30
Old fruit trees 8–10	40–50	15–20	8–10
Newly-planted fruit trees 4–5	20–25	8–10	4–5

which the shapes of treetops can be cut. Iceland moss, obtainable from gardens or flower shops, is washed in water and soaked in glycerine, so that it remains elastic and does not fall to pieces. The Iceland moss which is sold in model-building shops has too strong a colour for architectural model-making purposes. The loose inside of a loofah is suitable for larger-scale trees, and the outside for smaller-scale trees. Various sizes of scissors are suitable tools. Fragile parts should be sprayed with a fixative or hair spray. It is necessary to use a universal adhesive and, sometimes, paint. Once the tops of the trees have been cut, they can be attached to the correctly dimensioned tree trunks.

Trees made from artificial products
These are numerous possibilities:

- paper balls, wooden beads, peas, wooden balls, wooden dowels or round staves
- bottle-brushes
- expanded polystyrene balls, cork balls, methacrylate rods, foamed plastic weaves, mats of foamed plastic (for example, filter material for humidifiers)
- wire and sawdust, flower wire
- fine wire mesh
- steel wool
- nails

Spherical trees (1:1000 to 1:100) can be made from peas, wooden beads, expanded polystyrene, wood, wool,

211 Natural raw materials for the fabrication of trees: sheep's wool, alder cones, twigs, Iceland moss, loofahs, peas, thistle flowers. (*above*)

212 Artificial raw materials for the fabrication of trees: filter mats, sponges, foamed plastics, bottle-brushes, wire, steel wool, paper balls, methacrylate rods, electric cable, toothpicks. (*below*)

paper and steel wool. Trees can be made either with or without a trunk. Depending upon the nature of the model, and the ideas regarding materials to be used, the various spheres are either coloured, painted white, or left as they are.

Cone-shaped or cylindrical trees (1:500 to 1:100), are made from round rods (wood or methacrylate), bottle-brushes or plaited wire. The round rods are sanded either to a regular or an irregular shape with the bench sanding machine. They are then cut to the length re-quired. These trees can be made either with or without a trunk. Bottle-brushes, obtainable either from laborat-ory suppliers or hardware stores, are made in different sizes. They can be cut to the correct shape before they are assembled as part of the model.

Trees with an umbrella-like top (1:500 to 1:50), are made from either natural or artificial raw materials (see above). They can either be shaped freely or in the form of an umbrella. Wire, wire mesh, or rough fibre plastic matting (filters for humidifiers) are most widely used.

213 Model trees in the form of aluminium rivets, paper balls, wooden balls, round methacrylate rods, pins, alder and fir cones. (*above*)

214 Model trees made from foamed plastic, steel wool, paper balls, sanded wooden rods, larch cones, flower of a thistle plant. (*below*)

215   Model trees made from thorned twigs, wire trunk
with foamed plastic filter material, Iceland moss,
crumpled-up tissue paper, thyme twig, sheep's wool,
loofah. (*above*)

216   Model trees made from Iceland moss on toothpicks.
(*below*)

217 Pieces of a loofah on toothpicks.

218 Freely-sanded wooden balls on toothpicks to represent trees.

219 Steel wool as a hedge, poplar or ball-shaped tree.

220 Expanded polystyrene tree tops on toothpicks.

221 White painted paper balls, arranged in rows or forming free clusters.

222 Alder cones on pins.

Wire trees (1:200 to 1:50) are made as follows. A bundle of up to 12 wires, (flower wire or similar) is placed in a vice. The free ends are screwed into the chuck of a drilling machine and the wires are twisted slowly together. Depending upon the height of the tree and the diameter of the tree top, pieces can be cut off. The part which represents the tree top is opened up and bent to represent the various branches. Trees are made from fine wire mesh by cutting irregular shapes. The trunk is then made from either several thicknesses of wire or from a single wooden or metal rod. This is then pushed through the wire mesh. An interesting effect can also be achieved by the use of bits of carefully cut foam plastic matting, which is glued onto wooden pins.

Trees made from wire nails (1:1000 to 1:500) are used for small-scale models, to represent woods or clusters of trees. They are hammered into a landscape model in such a way that dense and sparse areas alternate. The tree tops can be represented by fixing either foam plastic mats or a fine wire mesh to the tops of the nails.

Finished trees

Finished trees are made commercially, and can be ordered from a catalogue. They are, however, mainly bought by model railway enthusiasts and may not be suitable for architectural models, as they may have the wrong colour, shape or degree of detailing. If these model trees are being considered, care must be taken that the scale dimensions are correct.

Only a few ways of fabricating trees have been shown here, although many more techniques can be used. There is virtually no limit to the methods which can be used to make model trees.

8.2 Human figures

Numerous human and animals figures can be purchased in specialist shops. Once again, it is essential to find out whether these highly-detailed figures will fit into the model.

217–222 Model trees at a scale 1:500. (*left*)

223 Foamed polystyrene ('Styrodur'), rough-cut and fixed to a pin. On the right the same thing, using balsa-wood instead.

224 Abstract figures, carved from foamed polystyrene and sprayed lightly, fixed with pins.

Preparation

- in very small-scale models, figures can be represented by caraway seeds, needles from fir trees or small wire nails (1:500)
- figures made from wooden profiles: look in periodicals or photograph albums for suitable pictures, and reduce them with a photocopier. The simplified silhouette is then traced onto the end of a wooden lath, which is shaped accordingly. The requisite number of figures can then be cut out from the lath (1:100 to 1:50)
- figures as silhouettes: various figures taken from photographs or prochures are enlarged or reduced with a photocopier, depending on the scale required. They are then glued onto carton and cut out (1:100 to 1:10)
- figures made from methacrylate sheeting: these are made in a similar way to the silhouette figures, but are glued onto thin methacrylate sheeting (1:100 to 1:10)
- figures made from pins, with paper clothing: this is a simple method of making abstract figures. Cut small and irregular areas from coloured or patterned paper. Fold them over and stick pins with round glass or black heads through them, (1:200 to 1:100)
- figures made from foamed plastics: these can be made just as quickly and easily as the paper figures mentioned above. Cut strips from the foamed plastic (extruded foamed EPS) 1 mm thick and, depending upon the sale, 1 to 2 cm wide. This is then cut into several tiny squares, and pins are stuck lengthwise through these squares. Using nail scissors, a human silhouette can now be cut out. This method is quick and particularly suitable for human figures in scales between 1:200 and 1:100
- figures made from strips of balsa-wood: slivers of different cross-sections and different lengths can be cut from a sheet of balsa. A pin is then pushed through

225 Printed paper (black/white or coloured), folded and cut to a rough shape, fixed with pins.

226 People and vehicles, 1:50, 1:100 and 1:200. All profiles are in hardwood, cut to the appropriate shape using a circular-saw, and trimmed to the correct lengths.
People at the scale of 1:200, barely 10 mm high, are subdivided by using a knife.

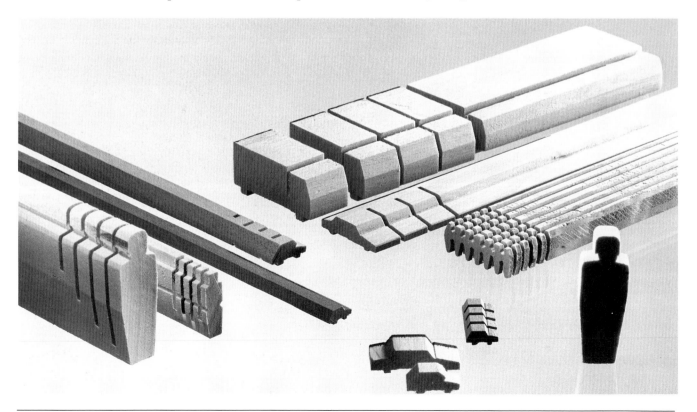

four or five of these pieces. The figure can then be painted. This method is most suitable for a scale of 1:100

– with larger models, figures can be made from 'Plasticine', clay or pieces of wire. It is even possible to produce the figures for larger models as jointed dolls. The single components should ideally be cubic in shape.

Reduction in size	1:50	1:100	1:200	1:500
Height of human being (1.75 m tall)	35 mm	18 mm	9 mm	3.5 mm

8.3 Vehicles

It is not necessary to produce specific models of cars. Almost any vehicle, in various scale variations and finished to perfection, can be purchased. It is, however, better for the architectural model to make the vehicles by hand. The silhouette of either a car or a lorry should be developed in the desired scale. Use a photograph, enlarged or reduced with a photocopier. The silhouette is then traced onto the end of a wooden lath. Using a circular-saw, the lath is worked to indicate the shape of the car or truck. Finally, the various cars are cut from this profiled lath. This degree of detail is quite adequate, as vehicles are only represented in small scales (1:500, 1:200, and less frequently, 1:100).

Vehicles	1:50	1:100	1:200	1:500
VW beetle: 4.1×1.5×1.5 m	82×30×30 mm	41×15×15 mm	20×7×7 mm	8×3×3 mm
Bus: 12×2.5×2.8 m	240×50×56 mm	120×25×28 mm	60×12×14 mm	24×5×6 mm
Railway carriage 26×3.5×4 m	500×70×80 mm	250×35×40 mm	125×17×20 mm	50×7×8 mm

8.4 Small details

Hand rails, railings, fences
These items can be soldered using wire (Section 6.4.4). They can also be bought in specialist shops (components for electronics, toys, parts for railway model-builders).

Furniture
For small-scale models (1:200, 1:100 and 1:50), benches and seats can be cut out from a profiled wooden lath in the same way as that described for vehicles. Small cubes, blocks and various timber and methacrylate pieces can be used to indicate furniture. Just as with all other scale-indicating items, furniture is not shown as any specific type, but is merely represented in size and overall shape.

227 Industrial plant, 1:500. Base plate: 13 mm sandwiched timber. Site and traffic areas in relief using 'Chromo' substitute carton. All buildings made from solid maple timber and sprayed. Filtration plant made from PVC. Chimney: 5 mm diameter aluminium tubes. Trees from turned beechwood dowels. The trees, like the technical plant components, serve to indicate the scale of the system.

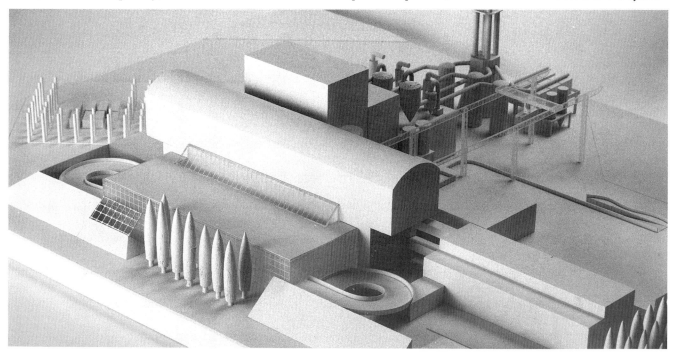

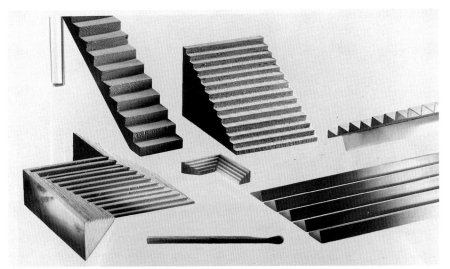

228 Staircase profiles, 1:500, 1:200, 1:100, 1:50.
Up to a scale of 1:100, it is possible to cut the staircase on a circular-saw as a solid profile. If the scale is 1:50 and larger, the single step profiles are cut separately as long laths, which are cut to the correct lengths, and then glued onto the staircase support.

229 Wide staircase. Model 1:20. Made from 1.6 mm aircraft plywood in layers around an assembly template. Assembled step-by-step and glued together. Five layers are equal to one step.

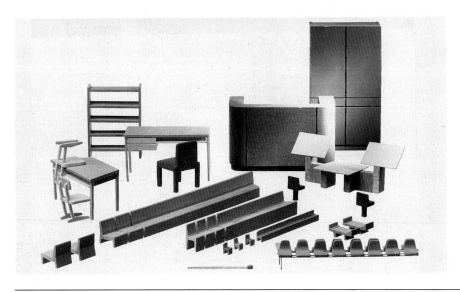

230 Furniture for internal room models in various scale dimensions. Bookcase 1:33, writing desk 1:20, school desk and stools 1:33, chair 1:100, stools 1:50 and 1:100, beds 1:100, drawing boards 1:50, sideboard and cupboard 1:20, chair shells on wire frame 1:50. Made from hardwood, using a circular-saw, partly as single entities and partly as lath profiles.

9 Using a Model to Develop the Overall Concept

A model acts differently from a drawing. Because of this, it should always articulate and describe the current ideas of the architect in a special way. It has the ability to represent a spatial concept and spatial relationships in three dimensions, and to document them as such. All this constitutes an enormous advantage over a mere drawing. In addition, it can show design characteristics, such as material, colour, relationship to its surroundings, etc., in a three-dimensional context.

It is not merely a representation of the architectural design, it has a design character of its own. It gives its own interpretation, which may correspond to or differ from that of the submitted plans. The intended interpretation and desired impression of the model must be clearly planned at the start, and properly prepared. In this way the appropriate methods may be selected, such as choice of construction materials.

A building model can exist on its own, i.e. without

231 Model, 1:50. 3 mm sandwiched EPS. Wire profiles, aluminium profiles, wire mesh. Structured methacrylate sheeting, thin wires, paints.

any integration into the urban or landscape environment. In such a case the scale and size of the model must be chosen to give the exact effect required. It is advisable in such cases to sketch out several schemes to find the best variant. This also gives a better indication of the materials needed, and how the model should be built. There are fewer intrinsically different methods of expression for single buildings than there are for interpreting their integration into the existing surroundings. The initial decision is between representation as a solid structure, as a combination of parts, or even of the parts on their own. Then it is necessary to decide whether the model is to be made from layers or linear elements, and how they are to be fitted together. Such a choice is initially independent of the material to be used, but is nevertheless the first step in the planning of the characteristics of the model. Several more decisions have to be made at this stage:

- is the model to be realistic or abstract?
- should its effect be quiet and sedate, or dynamic and exciting?
- should the model tone down or even obscure certain critical characteristics of the design for the people who are to judge the model (developer, committee, examiner), and if so, how should this be done?
- if some of the recommendations of the development plan have been exceeded, for example, the overall height of the building and the number of floors, should this be shown clearly, or should it be hidden by emphasizing the horizontal layers of the building? This makes it seem as if the height of the building is less than it is, without actually reducing its dimensions.
- should a very massive building structure be made to look less oppressive by building it more loosely and using transparent models?

The model-builder must ask himself or herself such questions constantly when selecting the methods to be employed in representing the structure. It is also necessary to reassess them during the fabrication process.

If a building is to be integrated with other buildings and/or a site, as in town planning models and models with a scale of 1:200, the builder of the model has to fix a section. This can correspond with the section shown in the plans, or it can, quite deliberately, possess other limits. The choice of the section and its position on the base plate of the model often determines the characterization of the model. For example, the building and its site are evenly surrounded by buildings which are arranged in such a way that the base plate is either square or rectangular. This forms a sedate and quiet frame for the model which is to be integrated. On the other hand, the model can be arranged differently: the section contour can be at an irregular angle, emphasizing certain lines and directions. The building may either fit in, or even show some contrasts. All this produces an exciting and dynamic effect. The same buildings that were integrated in a sedate way in the first example now appear in a completely different light.

The composition of base plate and choice of a suitable section, together with the way buildings and open areas are positioned upon it, determines and accentuates where emphasis is to be given. The shape and message to be conveyed by the model is further affected by the choice of the appropriate method of building the model, the materials used and the colour scheme selected.

If the model should accentuate the mass, volume and plastic shape of the building, an opaque, flat material should be chosen to emphasize the surface of the building structure. If, however, the model is to emphasize the correlation between the inside and the outside of the building, and how the building is actually constructed, different materials and methods are used. These should have graphic and surface characteristics to express sharp contrasts. This method of construction is recommended for the representation of 'colder' and more technological models, which give intrinsic details of their construction. When we wish to represent buildings in which the emphasis is on the way they fit in with their surroundings, such as old parts of a town, it is best to use a more solid construction, and show the surfaces in relation to the landscape around it.

Even when it is not necessary to represent the building's relationship with its surroundings, the aims of the builder, which may not yet have been clarified or fully finalized, should be expressed. It may perhaps only be necessary to present the design in an approximate and abstract way, to give the viewer the chance to interpret it more fully. Yet some other model-builder may wish to express the details of a building in the model with photographic precision and perfection. Nearly anything is possible.

Before a model is to be built, the job should be tackled in the following stages:

1 the scale is set
2 the section to be used, and the arrangement of the various parts, is fixed. The main aspects in such a case are the subdivision of the surface area, the centre of emphasis, and the directions from which the model should be viewed.
3 the effect required should be considered:
  - natural or abstract?
  - solid or transparent?

– coloured, monochrome or natural colour of materials used?
– linear (made from rods), flat (made from surfaces), solid (made from solid bodies)?
– rough or detailed?
– technological and cold, or friendly and warm?
– plastic or flat?
– informative, finalized, etc.?

4 final arrangements should be made regarding materials to be used and the colour scheme employed.

Only by learning to use the fabrication of a model to express the overall concept is it possible to start developing a distinctive 'model language'.

232 Building model, 1:100. Base plate: 16 mm sandwiched timber. Water surface: structured methacrylate on white background. Embankment: chipboard modelled with 'Polyfilla', and glued-on marble chippings. Bridge: solid lime timber covered with polystyrene. Large rock: solid lime timber, modelled with 'Polyfilla'. Loadbearing model of building is 3 mm thick sandwiched EPS, covered with mirror foil (double-sided glued surface). Façade made from clear methacrylate sheeting. Methacrylate framing, sprayed white. Closed façade surface made from white enamelled copper sheeting (double-sided adhesive foil). Surrounding external staircase: staircase profile from methacrylate, railing from silver wire. 'Nike' logo made from etched aluminium sheeting and attached to roof via a soldered loadbearing support unit.

Sources of Illustrations

O   = object
D   = designer
M   = model-builder
P   = photographer
IDM = University of Stuttgart, Institute of
       Draughtsmanship and Model-Making

1   O = Office tower, Frankfurt   D = Architects
    Prof. W. Knoll, C. Baum   M = W. Mierzwa
    P = H.–J. Heyer
2   O = Design seminar at IDM   D&M = Roland
    Wilhelm   P = H.–J. Heyer
3   O = Model–building seminar at IDM, 1989
    Tagblatt tower, Stuttgart (Architect: E. Otto
    Osswald 1928,   M = Nils Denker, Werner
    Kreuzholz   P = H.–J. Heyer
4   O = University of Kaiserslauten, Department of
    Chemistry (Architects: Heinle, Wischer and Partner)
    M = Martin Hechinger   P = Niko Koliusis
5   O = Office tower, Frankfurt   D = Architects
    Prof. W. Knoll, C. Baum   M = W. Mierzwa/
    M. Hechinger   P = H.–J. Heyer
6   O = Students' project at IDM, 1983/84
    M = group of students   P = H.–J. Heyer
7   O = Design seminar at IDM (under W. Everts,
    Dipl. Ing.), 1977   M = group of students
    P = H.–J. Heyer
8   O = Students' project at IDM (under Siegfried
    Albrecht, Michael Bendele)   M = Michael Bendele
    P = H.–J. Heyer
9   O = Students' project at IDM, 1982/83
    M = group of students   P = H.–J. Heyer
10 O = Students' project at IDM (under W. Everts,
    Dipl. Ing.)   P = H.–J. Heyer
11 O = Design project at IDM (under W. Everts,
    Dipl. Ing.), 1979/80   D&M = Joachim Hornbacher
    P = H.–J. Heyer
12 O = Study project at IDM, garden for study,
    1976/77   D&M = Barbalk, Huppert, Koenig
    P = H.–J. Heyer
13 O = Junior school, Stammheim, 1989; layout of
    garden; M.A. Fischer   D = Siegfried Albrecht
    M = M. Hechinger, S. Albrecht   P = H.–J. Heyer
14 O = Study project at IDM (under Siegfried
    Albrecht)   P = H.–J. Heyer
15 O = Study project at IDM, garden for study,

1976/77   D&M = Siegfried Gass   P = H.–J. Heyer
16 O = Study project at IDM (under Siegfried
    Albrecht)   D = Patrick Humpert   P = H.–J. Heyer
17 O = Study project at IDM (under Siegfried
    Albrecht)   P = H.–J. Heyer
18 O = Design at IDM (under W. Everts, Dipl. Ing.)
    D&M = Reinhard Koine   P = H.–J. Heyer
19 O = Study project at IDM (under Siegfried
    Albrecht)   D&M = Patrick Humpert
    P = H.–J. Heyer
20 O = Competition for Kleiner Schlossplatz,
    Stuttgart, 1985   D = Architect E. Herzberger
    M = M. Hechinger   P = H.–J. Heyer
21 O = Model–building seminar at IDM,
    Weissenhof Estate, Stuttgart, 1928
    D = Werkbund exhibition, 1928   M = work by a
    group   P = H.–J. Heyer
22 O = Design at IDM (under Prof. H. Buchwald)
    D&M = Joachim Kappeler   P = H.–J. Heyer
23 O = Model–building seminar at IDM, 1989,
    Weissenhof Estate, 1928   House of A.G. Schneck
    M = Paul Rothfischer   P = H.–J. Heyer
24 O = Design at IDM, 1989   D&M = Markus
    Hebel   P = H.–J. Heyer
25 O = University clinic, Regensburg, 1976
    D = Architects Heinle, Wischer and Partner
    M = M. Hechinger   P = H.–J. Heyer
26 O = Design at IDM, 1977/78   D&M = Winfried
    Klimesch   P = W. Knoll
27 O = Lower school, Stammheim, 1989
    D = Architect P. Hübner   M = M. Hechinger
    P = H.–J. Heyer
28 O = Office building, Karlsruhe, 1988
    D = Architect Prof. W. Knoll   M = C. Baum
    P = H.–J. Heyer
29 O = Study project at IDM (under Siegfried
    Albrecht)   P = H.–J. Heyer
30 O = University clinic, Essen   D = Architects
    Heinle, Wischer and Partner   M = M. Hechinger
    P = H.–J. Heyer
31 O = Seminar on casting technology (Dr
    A.P. Betschart), 1988/89   D&M = Uwe Geue
    P = H.–J. Heyer
32 O = Drawer column, 1989   D = Architect
    W. Knoll, colour treatment Susanne Schmidt
    M = M. Hechinger   P = H.–J. Heyer

33 O = Façade study D = Architect W. Knoll
M = M. Hechinger P = H.–J. Heyer
34, 35 P = H.–J. Heyer
36 O = Study project at IDM, 1967
V&M = C.B. Macher P = E. Seiferth
37 O = Study project at IDM, 1988
P = H.–J. Heyer
38 O = Design at IDM, 1988 D&M = Roland
Wilhelm P = H.–J. Heyer
39 O = Study project at IDM (under Siegfried
Albrecht), 1987 D&M = Max Stemshorn
P = H.–J. Heyer
40 O = Design at IDM, 1987 D&M = Wolfgang
Balbach P = H.–J. Heyer
41 P = H.–J. Heyer
42 O = Design at IDM (under W. Everts, Dipl. Ing.),
1977 D&M = Hans J. Schlecht P = H.–J. Heyer
43 P = H.–J. Heyer/M. Hechinger
44 O = Design at IDM, 1982 D&M = Christiane
Grimm P = H.–J. Heyer
45 O = Study project at IDM (under Siegfried
Albrecht) D&M = Monica Tachenberg
P = H.–J. Heyer
46 O = Study project at IDM (under Siegfried
Albrecht), 1987 D&M = Alfred Rein
P = H.–J. Heyer
47 O = Exhibition hall, Bonn, 1987
D&M = Architect H. Klumpp P = H.–J. Heyer
48 O = Study project at IDM (under Siegfried
Albrecht), 1987 D&M = Monica Tachenberg
P = H.–J. Heyer
49 O = Design at IDM (under W. Everts, Dipl. Ing.)
D&M = Franz Xaver Baier P = H.–J. Heyer
50 O = Study project at IDM, 1989 P = H.–J.
Heyer
51 P = H.–J. Heyer
52 P = H.–J. Heyer/M. Hechinger
53 O = Model–building seminar at IDM, 1987, State
Gallery, Stuttgart, 1983 (Architect J. Stirling)
M = Susanne Blumberg P = H.–J. Heyer
54 O = Design project at IDM, 1976/77
D&M = Siegfried Gergs P = W. Knoll
55 O = Diploma project (under Prof. Walter
Förderer), 1990 D&M = Werner Grosse
P = H.–J. Heyer
56 P = H.–J. Heyer/M. Hechinger
57 O = Model–building seminar at IDM, 1987
D&M = working party P = H.–J. Heyer
58 O = Model–building seminar, 1985, Le Corbusier
House, Weissenhoff Estate, 1927 M = Markus
Schaible P = H.–J. Heyer
59 O = Diploma project (supervised by Prof.
Dr. J. Joedicke) D&M = Andreas Edelmann
P = H.–J. Heyer

60 O = Diploma project at IDM, 1990 (Supervisor
Prof. W. Knoll) Fashion school, Stuttgart
M = W. Mierzwa P = H.–J. Heyer
61 P = H.–J. Heyer/M. Hechinger
62, 63 O = Study projects at IDM, 1989
P = H.–J. Heyer
64 P = H.–J. Heyer/M. Hechinger
65 D = Reinhard Rupf P = W. Knoll
66 P = H.–J. Heyer/M. Hechinger
67–70 P = H.–J. Heyer/Susanne Schmidt
71–76 P = H.–J. Heyer/M. Hechinger
77 P = H.–J. Heyer/M. Hechinger/Prof. W. Knoll
79 O = Model–building seminar at IDM (under
D. Worbs/M. Hechinger), 1989, Hugo Borst House,
1921 D = Architects E. Wagner and H. Wetzel
M = A. Geiselhard and H. Schiefer
P = H.–J. Heyer
80 O = Media houses for Russian newspapers in
Berlin D = Diploma project by Antje Krüger,
supervised by Prof. Uhl, University of Stuttgart,
1990 M = Antje Krüger P = H.–J. Heyer
81 D&M = Architect E. Herzberger
P = H.–J. Heyer
82 O = Apartment building and office block, 1986
D = Architects Prof. W. Knoll/E. Herzberger
M = M. Hechinger P = H.–J. Heyer
83 O = Music theatre, Linz D = Diploma project
by Caspar Baum, supervized by Prof. W. Knoll,
IDM, 1989 M = Caspar Baum P = H.–J. Heyer
84 M = N.N. P = H.–J. Heyer
85 O = Houses in Marburg, model-building
seminar at IDM (under M. Hechinger), 1990
D = O.M. Ungers M = D. Mueller/Aron
Weinsteiger P = H.–J. Heyer
86–91 M = W. Knoll/C. Baum P = H.–J. Heyer
92–94 M = W. Knoll/M. Hechinger
P = H.–J. Heyer
95 O = Diploma project, University of Stuttgart
P = H.–J. Heyer
96–100 P = H.–J. Heyer/M. Hechinger
101–104 Drawings by Prof. W. Knoll
105–109 P = H.–J. Heyer/M. Hechinger
110 M = N.N. P = H.–J. Heyer
111–119 P = H.–J. Heyer/M. Hechinger
120 O = Model–building seminar at IDM (under
D. Worbs, M. Hechinger), 1985, Weissenhof Estate,
Stuttgart, 1928 D = Architect J.J.P. Oud
M = Christoph Huettel P = H.–J. Heyer
121 O = Model–building seminar at IDM (under
M. Hechinger), 1985, Friedrich Wolf House 1928/29
D = Architect Richard Doecker M = R. Benz
A. Dorner P = H.–J. Heyer
122–127 P = H.–J. Heyer/M. Hechinger
128 O = Pavilion above entrance to underground

garage   D = Archiplan working party, Stuttgart
M = M. Hechinger   P = Norbert Daldrop
129–133   P = H.-J. Heyer/M. Hechinger
134   O = Clinic, Essen, 1976   D = Architects Heinle,
Wischer and Partner, Stuttgart
M = M. Hechinger   P = Niko Koliusis
135   O = Apartment building and office block,
Karlsruhe   D = Architect Prof. W. Knoll
M = M. Hechinger   P = H.-J. Heyer
136–141   P = H.-J. Heyer/M. Hechinger
142   O = Supply centre, Essen clinic, 1976
D = Architects Heinle, Wischer and Partner,
Stuttgart   M = M. Hechinger   P = H.-J. Heyer
143   O = Essen clinic, dormitories, 1976
D = Architects Heinle, Wischer and partner,
Stuttgart   M = M. Hechinger   P = H.-J. Heyer
144–146   P = H.-J. Heyer/M. Hechinger
147   O = Model–building seminar at IDM, 1988
(under M. Hechinger), Moller House, Vienna
D = Architect Adolf Loos   M = Oliver
Baumgaertner   P = H.-J. Heyer
148–150   P = H.-J. Heyer/M. Hechinger
151   O = Office block, Frankfurt, 1989
D = Architects Prof. W. Knoll, C. Baum
M = W. Mierzwa   P = H.-J. Heyer
152   O = Model–building seminar at IDM, (under
M. Hechinger), 1984, Villa Savoye
D = Le Corbusier   M = group of students
P = H.-J. Heyer
153–156   P = H.-J. Heyer/M. Hechinger
157–159   O = Competition: Red Cross Hospital,
Bad Cannstatt, 1989   D = Architects Eggert
and Partner, Stuttgart   M = M. Hechinger
P = H.-J. Heyer
160, 161, 164, 166, 169, 171, 172, 174, 175
P = H.-J. Heyer/M. Hechinger
162, 163, 165, 167, 168, 170   Schematic drawings by
C. Baum
173   O = Model–building seminar at IDM, 1978,
urban model   M = O. Baumgaertner
P = H.-J. Heyer
176   Model–building seminar at IDM, 1977
M = M. Geibel   P = H.-J. Heyer
177–182   P = H.-J. Heyer/M. Hechinger
183–188   O = Palm hothouse in the Exotic Garden,
Hohenheim   D = Steffi Neubert and Uschi
Brunner, University of Stuttgart, Institute for
Building Construction and Design; Prof. P.C. van
Seidlein, 1988   M = Steffi Neubert/Uschi Brunner
P = H.-J. Heyer
189   O = Model–building seminar at IDM, 1990
M = group of students   P = H.-J. Heyer
190   O = Model–building seminar at IDM, 1990
D&M = Margot Leinen   P = H.-J. Heyer

191   O = Medical Faculty, Goettingen, 1975
D = Architects Heinle, Wischer and Partner,
Stuttgart   M = M. Hechinger   P = Niko Koliusis
192   O = Bank building, Frankfurt   D = Architect
Prof. W. Knoll, 1988   M = M. Hechinger
P = H.-J. Heyer
193   O = Competition: State Museum of Fine Arts/
City Museum, Bonn, 1985   D = Architects
N. Moest, H. Klumpp   M = M. Hechinger
P = H.-J. Heyer
194   O = Department store, Breuninger, 1929/31,
Model–building seminar at IDM, 1989
D = Eisenlohr and Pfennig   M = Nikolaus
Tennigkeit   P = H.-J. Heyer
195   O = Concert hall on the lake, Diploma
project at IDM, 1989   D&M = N. Nasedy
P = H.-J. Heyer
196–198   O = Villa Savoye, 1929   D = Le Corbusier
M = M. Hechinger   P = H.-J. Heyer
199–201   O = Design of a kiosk   D = Architect Prof.
W. Knoll   M = H.W. Rhinow   P = E. Seiferth
202   O = Music theatre, Linz, 1989   D = Sabine
Sauter (supervised by architect Prof. W. Knoll)
M = Sabine Sauter   P = H.-J. Heyer
203   O = Stage set for Peter Weiss, *The pursuit and
murder of Jean Paul Marat*. Diploma project at IDM
1989 (supervised by Prof. W. Knoll)
D&M = Ulla Jansen   P = H.-J. Heyer
204   O = Gantry crane for storage sheds, Seminar
on special problems of building construction,
University of Stuttgart, Prof. P. Huebner
D = Architect S. Calatrava   M = Ch. Muth
P = H.-J. Heyer
205–209   O = Pavilion for Junior school,
Stammheim   D = Architect Prof. Peter Huebner
M = M. Hechinger   P = H.-J. Heyer
210, 211   P = H.-J. Heyer/Susanne Schmidt
212   P = H.-J. Heyer/M. Hechinger
213–215   P = H.-J. Heyer/W. Knoll/C. Baum
216   P = H.-J. Heyer/M. Hechinger
217–222   O = Model–building seminar at IDM
(under M. Hechinger)   P = H.-J. Heyer
223–225   P = H.-J. Heyer/W. Knoll/S. Schmidt
226   P = H.-J. Heyer/M. Hechinger/S. Schmidt
227   O = Competition: Refuse incineration plant,
Frankfurt, 1983   D = Architect L. Vidolovits
M = M. Hechinger   P = H.-J. Heyer
228–230   P = H.-J. Heyer/M. Hechinger
229   M = Werner Grosse   P = H.-J. Heyer
231   O = Pilot project at IDM (under E. Herzberger),
D&M = Nicola Haas   P = H.-J. Heyer
232   O = Tower for Nike, Linz, Diploma project at
IDM (under Prof. W. Knoll)   D&M = Gabriele
Schickedanz   P = H.-J. Heyer

Index

Page numbers in *italics* indicate illustrations.